FAMILIES THAT ABUSE

Diagnosis and Therapy

" And
Like It "

" ALot "

A Norton Professional Book

FAMILIES THAT ABUSE

Diagnosis and Therapy

Stefano Cirillo

Paola DiBlasio

TRANSLATED BY JOACHIM NEUGROSCHEL

W. W. NORTON & COMPANY / NEW YORK / LONDON

The text of this book was composed in Janson. Composition by
Bytheway Typesetting Services, Inc. Manufacturing by Haddon
Craftsmen, Inc.

Library of Congress Cataloging in Publication Data

Cirillo, Stefano.
[Famiglia maltrattante, English]
Families that abuse : diagnosis and therapy / Stefano Cirillo,
Paola di Blasio ; translated by Joachim Neugroschel.
p.   cm.
Translation of: La famiglia maltrattanta.
"A Norton professional book."
ISBN 0-393-70122-0
1. Child abuse—Treatment.   2. Family psychotherapy.   I. Di
Blasio, Paola.   II. Title.
RC569.5.C55C5713 /992 1991
616.85'822—dc20   91-44204   CIP

W.W. Norton & Company, Inc., 500 Fifth Avenue, New York, N.Y. 10110
W.W. Norton & Company, Ltd., 10 Coptic Street, London WC1A 1PU

1 2 3 4 5 6 7 8 9 0

PREFACE TO THE ENGLISH EDITION

THE SOBERING PROBLEM OF family violence directed at children demands a response from society mandated with the protection of children; the predicament of children and their families experiencing this pain requires a family-based clinical approach to their treatment. This book argues for the absolute necessity for both protection and treatment of abused children and their families and makes a powerful case for harnessing these two functions together. It is a pragmatic and scholarly review, informed by the commitment of clinicians working with abusive families who reveal their work through their practical approaches to numerous family predicaments, and it is refreshingly honest about the dilemmas encountered in this work. Often, the work of family therapy is situated in the real world of conflicting mandates, with pressures from courts, agencies, schools and professional bodies, all of which may constrain our therapeutic choices. In this book, Stefano Cirillo and Paola DiBlasio tackle such workaday problems head on.

I have followed the work of the authors in their collaborations together and with others in Italy. We share common concerns about the well-being of children and their families, the effective and ethical conduct of family therapy, as well as inspiration from Mara Selvini Palazzoli as a mentor for family studies. Cirillo and DiBlasio have both clearly learned a great deal from the seminal work of their well-known teachers in Milan but have also made original contributions in new areas, including Cirillo's books on foster families (1986) and on conducting therapy in nontherapeutic contexts (1990), and DiBlasio's contribution to a volume about conducting family therapy in larger systems (1987), as well as her work on family violence (1988a, 1988b). It is a pleasure to see more of their work available to English readers. As a child psychiatrist dealing daily with allegations of abuse and the consequences for both children and their families, I find this book a useful contribution. As director of an adolescent day treatment program located in a community high school, my practice of family therapy is enveloped in the kinds of multisystem issues the authors have carefully dissected. Careful attention to families who find themselves at the nexus of different systems offers the richness of greater reach into their lives. It also provides an opportunity to address and resolve conflicts between providers that this can engender.

Families That Abuse belongs to a whole new generation of family work: using a systemic perspective with a commitment to treating families, it addresses a clinical problem with serious symptoms and consequences (not just structural malalignments or systemic perturbations). Drawing from the clinical insights of Mara Selvini Palazzoli and her colleagues at the New Center for Family Studies in Milan, the authors use this as a launching pad for wider investigations. In this work, Cirillo and DiBlasio live up to the promise of Mara Selvini Palazzoli's early prediction: "Family therapy is the starting point for the study of ever wider social units" (1974, p. 241).

The authors venture both wider and deeper than earlier works in family therapy in their analysis of families that abuse. This is exemplified by their examination of two key areas: mandated treatment and family diagnosis. In the second chapter on mandated contexts for therapy, the authors describe the problems of coordinating the different mandates of therapy and of social control. I recall many conversations with family therapists in such enlightened centers as the Institute of Psychiatry of the University of London and the Institute of

Community and Family Psychiatry of McGill University in Montreal that floundered on this issue and interventions that fell short of the workable solutions offered in this book. Some clinicians seem hampered by practical problems such as communicating across agencies (with ethical and legal justifications such as client consent for disclosure); others seem to display systemic rigidity or what may be called "hardening of the categories."

In their recent book on *Milan Systemic Family Therapy* (1987), Boscolo and associates reveal a cavalier attitude towards functions of health care, which they call "social control." As I argued in my review of the more recent work of different members of the original Milan group of the 1970s (DiNicola, 1990), their proposed solution is facile ("there is no problem as long as the therapist is clear about which hat she is wearing, a 'therapist' hat or a 'social control' one," Boscolo et al., 1987, p. 24). Family therapy has been avoiding such confrontations with reality by pretending that you can reframe the situation (passing the problem to someone else) or by complaining about the coercive nature of health care or social services (as a critical outsider or a subversive rebel within such systems). What impresses me most about *Families That Abuse* is the honest attempt made to directly solve such problems in a way that is practical and also advances our theoretical notions of how therapy proceeds. For example, Cirillo and DiBlasio clearly state in a way that few strategic therapists say publicly that paradoxical interventions are contraindicated where dependent and vulnerable family members may become victims.

Employing the seminal work of Mara Selvini Palazzoli and her colleagues on family games, the authors offer an overview of the diagnosis of the abusive family (Chapter IV) and the games typical of abusive families (Chapter V). North American workers in the family field have become more genuinely concerned with issues of meaning and authenticity in the co-construction of the therapeutic story with the family in treatment. Such concerns may make the language of the Milan team sound overly concerned with games and secrets, power and strategies. Yet the notion of the family game, specifically defined for clinical contexts as the relational patterns of a family, offers great explanatory power in its ability to convey rich amounts of information in a schematic way. This is appealing because it suggests that the messy interactions that we only glimpse parts of in therapy have an underlying order or meaning. Indeed, I believe that this use of the notion of family games is the most important new approach to the problem of family diagnosis since Salvador Minuchin's structural model of family boundaries and the enmeshment/disengagement spectrum he posited.

I can only conclude by warmly inviting the reader to enter this book, becoming its real author by deconstructing the text and creating her own solutions to the problems of abused children and their distressed families.

Vincenzo F. DiNicola, M.D.
Director, Family Therapy Training
Assistant Professor of Child and Adolescent Psychiatry
University of Ottawa
Ottawa, Ontario, Canada
November 1991

CONTENTS

FOREWORD

THE AUTHORS OF THIS STUDY handed me the manuscript of their book last summer, at the start of the holidays. I can still recall how stunned I was upon reading it, and I can imagine how stunned a good number of my colleagues will be. This book shocked me by making me aware of two factors that concerned me personally. For one thing, I realized that when I had first gotten into family therapy, I had talked about the context and the "shifts" from the context, but without completely understanding them or dealing with an essential consequence. Which result? That we can achieve therapeutic effects in any context, even one that clashes—as court-mandated therapy does—with the common "ideology" of the spontaneous request for help. Our only basic requirement is that we deliberately remain inside the context, adjusting our modus operandi to the rules and boundaries that define the context and make it meaningful. This requirement is marvelously demonstrated here, precisely because the authors present it as the first step they took in overcoming a tangle of errors, which they unhesitatingly describe.

This leads to my second realization. As I read the manuscript, I felt certain that I, too, at that time, in their place, would have done the same. Conditioned as I am by both my training and my work, first as a psychoanalyst, then as a family therapist in a private context (which is ruled by the request for help), I would have found myself in the same quandary. I, too, would have behaved ambiguously with parents; I would have felt almost embarrassed about virtually representing the court of law. I, too, would have taken a long time to understand that mandated therapy has its raison d'être. Its inescapable goal is the immediate protection of the child from further abuse; yet, precisely because of its temporary nature, this context does not prevent the judge from relying on expert advice for diagnosing the recovery prospects of the parents and determining the possible implementation of therapy.

Mandated context are instituted specifically for protecting *helpless* members of society, who can in no way defend themselves against violence; thus, the *reluctance* to adjust constructively to this context is something to ponder. Indeed, this reluctance is expressed in fairly similar ways by directly or indirectly abusive parents, by children who are victims of violence, and by the professionals who are supposed to deal with them. Stefano Cirillo and Paola Di Blasio show us how these parents react when confronted with unequivocal evidence of the violence that they have inflicted on a child. As a rule, they strenuously deny any wrongdoing, they blurt out excuses and justifications, and they even come up with bombastic ideological rationales. Furthermore, with rare exceptions, the parent who is not directly abusive engages in a collusion of silence with the abusive parent. Even battered children under seven or eight years of age keep silent about the abuse they have suffered, as if trying to protect their parents and their own relationship to them — at the cost of repeatedly exposing themselves to serious danger. And finally, there is the professional assigned to tackle the problem: His or her behavior is no different from that of these children and their parents, but it is a lot harder to explain. Hoping to win over the parents, he wraps himself in a mantle of nonpunitive understanding; but in his self-delusion, he simply minimizes the gravity of the facts, causing serious delays and neglecting his urgent and sacrosanct duty to shield the child against any risk of further maltreatment.

It's quite a shock to see the repetition of such behavior in the three categories of people playing such different roles in the drama of child abuse: parents, children, professionals. Nor are we satisfied with the diverse explanations of the possible reasons for their behaviors. Thus, the work of the Center for the Abused Child and the Treatment of Family Crises (CBM in the Italian acronym) has inaugurated a welcome shattering of old sociocultural conditions.

But let's get to the authors' description of the chronological sequence of their insights, as summed up here:

1. The primary goal of the Juvenile Court order is the urgent removal of the child from his/her family and, thereby, from any risk of further violence.
2. This ruling is the only effective tool for reaching this type of family, which, characteristically, never asks for help.
3. This approach can motivate the parents and bring about their genuine collaboration not only because they want to get back their child(ren), but also through various requirements in therapy. These are indispensable:

    a. The therapist must agree, explicitly and unreservedly, with the ruling handed down by the Juvenile Court; in so doing, he must have no mental reservations whatsoever and he must be absolutely convinced that the minor's protection has top priority.

    b. The therapist must be able to motivate the parents to change their relationship by reconstructing, and showing them at an early point, the tragic modalities of the complex interactive game in which they're entangled—a game that normally involves three generations and leads to abusive behavior.

It must be emphasized that, in their therapeutic work with abusive families, the authors have certainly benefited from using the metaphor of the "game." The relational organization of a family is not a static structure; rather, it is a living, dynamic process that reacts to events and evolves over time. The emergence of unacceptable behavior is therefore linked to the specific evolution of family relations: It results from a game, or interactive process, and we therapists have to try and *retrace its development*, step by step, reconstructing the history of the relational organization of the family in which such behavior erupts. If we hope to succeed as quickly as possible in "fascinating" and involving the family by presenting the "historical" reconstruction of the game that conditions its members, we need a great deal of training. The authors of this volume went through their training by personally participating in the family research that has been conducted for years now at the Nuovo Centro per lo Studio della Famiglia (New Center for the Study of the Family) directed by Mara Selvini Palazzoli. Cirillo has been practicing therapy there since 1982, and Di Blasio was there from 1981 to 1985, working with Giuliana Prata. Hence, their book includes concrete personal testimony resulting from numerous case histories and treatments.

In confronting their own painful stories within the relatively short span of an investigation, many unfortunate parents became cooperative when they sensed that the therapists were genuinely interested. The helpfulness of these parents, as you will see when reading this book, *always* involved the inclusion of their families of origin in the investigation. This meant dealing with their intense and frustrating relationships with one or both parents, and their continuing rivalries with and keen jealousies of the "favored" sibling. Here, too, as Murray Bowen has correctly asserted in regard to families with schizophrenic children, it apparently takes three generations to inflict violence on a child.

Nor can we, as you will likewise see in this book, exclude from the reconstruction of the family process a possible active contribution from the victim himself, who is sometimes more precocious than adults imagine. It is difficult to remain outside the game. It is difficult, say, to keep witnessing a conflict between parents day after day without participating in it, without taking sides. From his crib, the child, no longer an infant, observes everything happening around him. He listens to his grandmother's complaints, he overhears his mother's endless telephone calls, he absorbs his uncles' and aunts' mordant comments. . . . Little by little, the child is drawn into the game and he forms his own picture of it; he even grows convinced that the situation involves a victim, someone to defend. Gradually, he too makes his moves in the game. If the therapists remain unaware of this possibility, they risk losing sight of the child as active participant and not just passive recipient of actions perpetrated by others; thus, the therapists may overlook an important therapeutic potential.[1]

The work done so far by Cirillo and Di Blasio (and the work still to be done—for this book shows only the first stage) has many important features to its credit. However, in concluding this foreword, I want to emphasize what I regard as the chief merit of their book: the fact that they have understood, and done their best to make others understand, the necessity of remaining true to the overall context in which they happen to be operating. As a result, any context that can be defined as nontherapeutic may offer the therapist indispensable possibilities of therapeutic action—so long as the therapy, which is meant to produce desirable changes in relationships, sticks to the following guidelines. It must not only take the context into account, but also utilize the marks and rules (not to be confused with lazy, rigid, and obsolete habits) as valid propulsors. Experiments of this sort—that is, attempts at thoroughly testing the resources of contexts other than the therapeutic one—have emerged in institutional environments—nor could it be otherwise. Let me list a few of those experiments, merely to give you some idea of the vast range of possibilities. Think of the field of social work for senior citizens. In regard to the demand for places in hospitals and old age homes, an array of expedient and up-to-date information can sometimes inspire the professional, who ignores only the rigid red tape, to come up with some relational improvements that might otherwise not have occurred. Or think of the diagnostic and evaluative context, with its

---

1. In this connection, see Diana and Louis Everstine, *People in Crisis* (New York: Brunner/Mazel, 1983). The Everstines never even contemplate the possibility of the child's active participation in the conflict of the parental couple.

goal of making referrals. Here too, the request for a referral can be used by the therapist to tactfully investigate the underlying relational causes; he or she can take advantage of the opportunity to work toward a change in certain family relationships. Or think of the very common demand for financial help. For the attentive therapist, this may be the tip of an iceberg, hinting at greater and more serious needs, which people cannot express if they know nothing about psychotherapists or psychotherapy.[2]

In this way, the tremendous work and effort described in this book can be regarded as harbingers of a new trend, which, by and large, must still be developed.

This new direction must be taken not only by therapists, but by social workers in general—especially in institutions. Today, we must expect less and less that people, impelled by *authentic* motives, seek help *spontaneously*. It is time we became, first of all, experts in motivating people to change their relationships if they have a great need to do so. And this means being capable not only of inducing the change, but also of making the need for it emerge.

Mara Selvini Palazzoli
Milan
March 1989

2. Since 1982, Stefano Cirillo has been working on this line of investigations with a group of professionals affiliated with different kinds of institutions. Their experiences were recently elaborated on by the participants themselves and were gathered in a book entitled, *Il cambiamento nei contesti non terapeutici* (How to implement changes in nontherapeutic contexts), Cirillo, 1990.

ACKNOWLEDGMENTS

THIS BOOK IS THE FRUIT of our experience in a long collective labor with a large group of friends and colleagues, some of whom are still part of our team.

We owe our primary gratitude to all of them, whose names and efforts are described in our text. Among them, we are particularly thankful to Teresa Bertotti, Marinella Malacrea, and Alessandro Vassalli, with whom we have long shared the daily toil of working with families, and to whom we are also indebted for their close perusal of our manuscript and for their useful suggestions. We are also thankful to Tito Rossi, president and "senior" friend of our Center, who has warmly encouraged us in our undertaking.

Next, we owe gratitude to our teacher, Professor Mara Selvini Palazzoli, who patiently reviewed our entire manuscript step by step, guiding us with her unique advice. Likewise, her colleagues and our friends, Matteo Selvini and Anna Maria Sorrentino, have helped us by reading the manuscript and making various suggestions, for which we are grateful. We are also grateful to Francesca Ichino Pellizzi, attorney-at-law, and Giovanna Picinali Ichino, magistrate, who, with their expertise, have verified the legal references in our text.

Finally, we would like to express our thanks to Guiliana Mauro Paramithiotti for her invaluable contribution in typing the manuscript.

FAMILIES THAT ABUSE

Diagnosis and Therapy

I | THE CONTEXT OF EXPERIENCE

Founding the Help Center for Abused Children and Families in Crisis (CAF)

IN 1979, IN THE CITY OF MILAN, an independent association was formed, the Centro di aiuto al bambino maltrattato e alla famiglia in crisi—Help Center for Abused Children and Families in Crisis (CAF). Its goal was to prevent all child abuse, to help and support minors who are victims of violence, mistreatment, and abandonment, and to help and support their families as well. Toward this end, as written in the association charter, the founders wanted to create and administer a center for welcoming children who were victims of physical and/or mental abuse, violence, and abandonment. They planned to supply swift emergency aid, as requested or authorized by the court or some other authority, by the social services, or in response to complaints by private citizens. They also intended to provide therapy and support for parents in crisis and for those with serious mental or social problems in regard to their children.

The association, organized by Ida Crane Borletti, was the brainchild of a group of private citizens who, long active in Milan's social health assistance scene, had made significant achievements in this area. This is demonstrated by the fact that the second signer of the

1

CAF charter was Francesca Ichino Pellizzi, a lawyer and a cofounder of the earlier CAM (Centro ausiliario per i problemi minorili presso il Tribunale per i minorenni—Auxiliary Center for the Problems of Minors attached to the Juvenile Court). Among its tasks, the CAM promoted and implemented foster care for minors, placing countless children in foster care even when this institution was still barely used by the public services.

While all 12 founders of the CAF were private citizens, some of them also had positions in public institutions, thereby giving the Center an immediate prominence in Milan. These people included Adolfo Beria d'Argentine and Gilberto Barbarito, at the time the presiding and assistant judges of Milan's Juvenile Court; university professors like the pediatrician Biagio Carletti, the psychologist Fulvio Scaparro, the jurist Pietro Schlesinger. A further important link between the nascent CAF and the community was the fact that one of its cofounders was Ernesto Caffo, secretary of the Italian Association for the Prevention of Child Abuse (AIPAI: Associazione italiana per la prevenzione dell'abuso all'infanzia). Given this overall clout, it is understandable that the municipal authorities of Milan hailed this initiative—the first of its kind in Italy. Showing great sensitivity in grappling with the largely underestimated phenomenon of child abuse, the city leaders gave the Center a building (which already housed a nursery) and signed an agreement with the CAF, which began operating in January 1981.

The Response of the City of Milan and the Survey of Abuse

The staff of the Center had the following makeup: two foster couples in charge of the Residential Care Unit for minors; two social workers; and three family therapists as the psychosocial unit.[1] In the

---

1. The foster couples were Maurizio and Nadia Agape, and Domenico and Floriana Sala. The social workers were Fausta Fano and Edmea Pincelli. The therapists were Bruna Bianchi, Stefano Cirillo, and Marinella Malacrea.

months prior to the opening of the Center, the staff members went through a formative training under Fulvio Scaparro; its subject was child abuse and how to deal with it. During this training, one of the key items in the CAF program grew more and more salient: the goal of becoming an auxiliary to, but not a substitute for, the social health services.

As a result, no sooner did the CAF staff members begin to present their program to the network of services in order to establish cooperation than they were confronted with the task of identifying the scope of their own activities. They had to forestall the danger that this new agency might be indiscriminately consulted by the social services in regard to all complex, acute, or chronic welfare cases. This was a justifiable worry, given that the Center had only a few beds for emergencies and that, in those days even more than today, the capacity of Milan's emergency shelters was far below the city's needs.

For this reason, the CAF made a point of defining as clearly as possible child abuse in families—the chief object of the Center's activity. The definition of abuse on which the CAF decided to focus had been formulated several years earlier by the Council of Europe at the Fourth Colloquium of Criminology, held in Strasbourg in 1978 (Council of Europe, 1981). According to this definition, "abuse" meant "any acts or omissions that seriously disturb the child, endanger his or her bodily integrity, physical, emotional, intellectual, or moral development, and whose manifestations are neglect and/or injuries of a physical and/or mental and/or sexual nature by a family member or by anyone else who is in charge of the child."

Thus, cases of child abuse within a family may be classified as follows: physical mistreatment, in which the family members subject the minor to any aggression with any physical consequences (such as cutting the skin, ocular or internal injuries, fractures, burns, permanent injuries, death); sexual molestation, in which the minor is forced by family members into sexual acts to which the child cannot knowingly consent; serious neglect, in which the minor suffers the effects of the family's acts of neglect or omission in regard to his or her physical and/or mental needs (clothing not adequate to climatic conditions; neglect in regard to health, hygiene, or food; lack of schooling; malnutrition, etc.); psychological abuse, in which the minor is the victim of repeated verbal violence or damaging psychological pressure—this latter category includes all those situations of conflictual parental separation in which minors are patently exploited in the parental conflict, with an obvious and noticeable impact on their emotional balance.

Consistent with this definition, during the CAF's first 11 months of activity (January through November 1981), it received 39 "proper" referrals—that is, cases filtered from the general mass of initial referrals. During the first ten months of the following year (January through October 1982), the number of "proper" referrals zoomed up to 109, so many that the Center managed to take over only 46 of these cases and was forced to turn down the rest. Quite a few were rejected because of geographic problems; referrals had begun coming in from the surrounding province, from other cities, and even from other regions—a situation testifying to the shortage of available resources. During the following year, 1983, the number of child abuse cases that the CAF was able to accept reached 56 in the first five months alone! Obviously, this dizzying increase in demand could not be due to any wildfire spread of the tragedy of abuse. A more likely explanation lies in the nature of this phenomenon, which is carefully concealed by the participants and obscured to some extent by the indifference and denial of the observers. At last, the submerged portion of the iceberg was starting to come to light.

The Duplication of Services for Child Abuse: The Birth of the CBM

At this point, because of the increasing awareness of the vast scope of child abuse, the City Hall, in the person of Attilio Schemmari, the then municipal councilor for welfare and social assistance, instituted a special municipal agency devoted to this problem. This new agency would have two functions: as an observatory, to coordinate the survey of child abuse in families; and as a laboratory, to define and try out appropriate techniques for dealing with such cases.

In June 1984, several members of the CAF staff[2]—psychologists, social workers, educators—established a cooperative known as the CBM (Centro per il bambino maltrattato e la cura della crisi familiare—Center for the Abused Child and the Treatment of Family Crises). Then, in April 1985, the City Hall entrusted the CBM with running its own agency. This made the CBM the first public agency in Italy to tackle child abuse. It supplemented the work of the CAF, which continued to operate as a private agency in Milan and the adjacent communities, so that the North Italian metropolis now had two specialized centers.

Within the network of Milan's public health services, the CBM does not have jurisdiction over all cases of child abuse; this would be not only quantitatively impossible, but, above all, inconsistent with its program. For some time now, regional services have been developing the necessary skills for dealing with families that, when suffering a crisis, reveal distress symptoms analogous to those of abusive families. However, the particular complexity of such cases has highlighted the need for a specialized agency with two functions. It would operate as a *checkpoint*, gathering the experiences of the basic and second-level agencies; and it would operate as a *research center*, capable of developing its own experiences in regard to particularly complex cases referred by district agencies: that is, dramatically acute cases or, vice versa, chronic situations.

On the basis of such experiences—its own and those of others—the CBM has worked out specific procedures for treating child abuse cases, and it has conveyed those methods to other agencies for their

2. Maurizia Azzoni (social worker), Floriana Battevi (secretary), Stefano Cirillo (psychotherapist), Teresa Di Bari (educator), Paola Di Blasio (psychotherapist), Anna Frigerio (social worker), Laura Gabbana (educational psychologist), Graziano Gatta (educator), Alessandro Vassalli (psychotherapist and director). They were joined by Tito Rossi (current president) and, later on, Teresa Bertotti (social worker), Marinella Malacrea (psychotherapist), Virginio Marchesi (psychologist). One year ago, Elena Fontana (social worker) replaced Maurizia Azzoni.

own implementation. Our Center has shared its knowledge in consultations, which any agency can request when directly confronted with an abuse situation. Moreover, the CBM team has participated in city seminars and conventions, at which we inform the various Milanese institutions about our approaches and methods and the results we have obtained.[3]

In order to further the CBM's commitment to deepening its own knowledge of technique and theory, our team is backed up by a scientific committee. At the moment, its members are: Gilberto Barbarito, the current presiding judge of Juvenile Court, as well as several university professors representing the disciplines pertaining to the field of child abuse treatment: Bianca Barbero Avanzini, sociologist; Giuseppe Masera, pediatrician; Assunto Quadrio, psychologist; Giuseppe Vico, teacher of education; and Odette Masson, a pediatric neuropsychiatrist and head of the Swiss Association against Child Abuse. Her operational model in child abuse cases (Masson, 1981) served as a valuable guide for our team when we were first starting out.

Organization of the CBM: The Residential Care Unit

In order to cope with its own tasks, the CBM set up a secretariat as well as a Residential Care Unit and a psychosocial team; these latter two units are coordinated by a clinical psychologist who functions as overall director. The Residential Care Unit can shelter abused minors, or those at risk of abuse, as soon as Juvenile Court requires their immediate and temporary removal from their parents, and as soon as the City Social Service, to whose care the children are entrusted, feels it is appropriate to refer them to the CBM. Our Care Unit can shelter as many as ten minors up to 12 years of age (the inclusion of adolescents would involve very different needs and thus

3. So far, two conferences have taken place. The first one, in April 1985, inaugurated the Center's activity; the topic was "Child Abuse in Families and Operative Protection of Minors." The topic of the second conference (November 1987) was "Intervention in Incest Cases."

place too great a strain on our resources). The Care Unit can also house a parent whenever this seems useful; after all, it might be harmful to remove very small children from their mothers (many of whom are likewise abused by their husbands), and it would also be helpful to observe the child-mother relationship. The Care Unit has four residential workers whose work is coordinated by an expert in educational psychology; they are assisted by a cleaning lady and two conscientious objectors (performing alternative service).

The staff runs the Care Unit as a "therapeutic environment" for coping with many different demands. Chronologically, the first goal of the residential workers is to help the child, already traumatized by abuse, to cope with the stress of being removed from his or her parents and being placed in unfamiliar surroundings. In this connection, we must remember that several procedures may take place, even in emergencies, as soon as the child is removed—say, by the police—and brought to our center to wait until Juvenile Court issues its first temporary order. Perhaps the removal has occurred at night, and the child is frightened, bewildered, and depressed. While staying at the Residential Care Unit, children maintain a link to their normal reality by continuing to attend their regular schools, to which the hospice provides transportation.

The second goal of the Care Unit requires a greater time span: The staff helps the child through the process of working through with what has happened. With great difficulty, the child has to find his bearings in regard to the dramatic event of which he is the protagonist: abuse by people on whom he depends both materially and emotionally—his parents—and whom he loves and simultaneously fears. At the Care Unit, residential workers also help the child to understand everything happening in him and around him: his being cared for by other people, the entry into his life of strangers (the Juvenile Court judge, the social worker) who, despite their rather vague identities, wield so much power in determining his life now and in the near future.

The third goal of the Care Unit throughout the period of sheltering the child is observation. First and foremost, the staff observes the child's mental and physical condition. The child undergoes a thorough medical examination, including, if appropriate, a gynecological examination for girls, and the full range of his behavior is assessed. Furthermore, during telephone conversations with and visits from his parents, who can come at specific hours on alternating days, his relationship to them is closely monitored. That is why a residential worker is always present during such telephone calls and visits. In this way, the worker can prevent the parents (who are often themselves confused and frightened) from acting unsuitably towards the child. Above all, in studying these contacts, the worker can collect a huge amount of information about the parent-child interaction. All these data are incorporated in a diagnostic report, which, as we will see later on, is sent to the judge; the diagnosis integrates the psychosocial team's evaluation of the family's recovery prospects.

Naturally, the Residential Care Unit personnel is not limited to noting the quality of the parents' behavior toward the child. Rather, the staff members try to direct the parents toward gradually adopting more appropriate conduct—that is the fourth goal of our Care Unit. As you may have guessed, while our Care Unit aims at the prompt reception of abused children, their stays are seldom brief. Often they remain for more than three months, and in some cases as long as a year, depending on how much time is required for the always complex process of diagnosing a family. Broadly speaking, the child leaves the Care Unit when the psychosocial team has formulated the diagnosis and the prognosis of the family's chances of recovery. The judge reaches her decision after perusing this diagnosis and prognosis as well as the report from the responsible City Social Service. She can now mandate any of several possibilities: If the prognosis is positive, the child may return to her family; but, if the prognosis is negative, the child may be removed once and for all from her family and put up for adoption. There is a third alternative: So long as the prognosis is positive, the temporary removal period may be extended if it is necessary for the parents to undergo treatment in the absence of the child. In the latter instance, the responsible social service, together with the Center team, determines the new provisional arrangement that best fits the needs of the child, who is usually placed with a foster family or sometimes in another Care Unit.

For this reason, the minors staying at the CBM are seldom resettled (for instance, put in an institution or in diagnostic custody) so long as the diagnosis of and prognosis for the family are incomplete (Cirillo, 1988). Our reason for keeping the child at our Care Unit during the diagnostic period is simply to prevent him from being dismally shuttled from one temporary situation to another, equally temporary one, while waiting for the final evaluation to indicate whether we ought to return him to his family or find some other solution (i.e., provisional foster care, a different Care Unit, or adoption). On the negative side, this waiting period involves prolonged Care Unit stays for these children; because of this slow turnover of guests, we are often unable to accept new referrals.

The Psychosocial Team

The second unit at the CBM is the psychosocial team, which is composed of two social workers and three family therapists (two psychologists, who are the authors of this book, and a child neuropsychiatrist).

This team can take on about 30 families—a case load exceeding the ten-bed capacity of our Care Unit. As a result, some of the children are put up in other places, with which our team works out a collaborative plan. In a few less serious situations, the court may not order a child's removal from his family. Instead, the judge assigns custody of her to the city of Milan: The social service is to act as monitor, and the family unit, as in the previous instances, has to report to the CBM for evaluation and possible treatment.

Each family is allocated to a mini-team made up of two therapists and a social worker. This mini-team works closely with the staff of either our Care Unit or one of the other care units for children, as well as with the district social worker responsible for the case.

The CBM's psychosocial team, as we will see, has two functions: diagnosis of (and prognosis for) the abusive family's chances of recovery and therapy in cases of a positive prognosis.

The Theoretical Approach to Abuse and Our Reference Model

In our approach to child abuse cases, the operational model that we have adopted for the stages of both diagnosis and therapy focuses more on the articulated and complex family dynamics underlying the violence than on the problems of individuals viewed in isolation. The CBM team has come to believe that manifestations of neglect, physical violence, and/or sexual molestation are symptoms of a pathology attacking the overall functioning of the family in question (Di Blasio, 1988a). Consistent with this assumption, our goal is not just to understand the reasons for the maltreatment, but also to modify the dysfunctional patterns in which the violence is rooted. Thus, our ultimate objective is to enable the family to recover its own child-raising functions.

At present, the focus of attention on the family, or rather on the family game (Selvini Palazzoli et al., 1985, 1989), seems to be the most suitable choice for tackling the complexity of a phenomenon with so many individual, cultural, and social intricacies. If we briefly analyze the results obtained in this field, we see that since 1962, when Kempe and his colleagues identified the "battered child syndrome," a huge number of studies have been done in this area. The keen interest triggered by this topic is documented not only by this wealth of research, but also by the appearance of specialized periodicals, the most important being *Child Abuse and Neglect International Journal* (the organ of the ISPCC, the International Society for Prevention of Cruelty to Children).

Nevertheless, the experts have hitherto failed to reach an adequate agreement on the psychological mechanisms at the heart of this phenomenon. Family violence is often regarded in terms of a paralyzing stereotype: Many people link it exclusively to the deviance typical of socially and culturally deprived milieus, with psychopathological consequences that can be intuited but seldom defined. There are certainly few follow-up studies documenting the long-term effects of abuse. Likewise, it is hard to compare different types of violence, as well as their frequency and duration. All those obstacles may partly explain the caution exercised in more explicitly recognizing the full pathogenic thrust of such cases (Bandini & Gatti, 1987). Furthermore, Bowlby (1984) points out a tendency in certain sectors of classical psychoanalysis to ignore or minimize the impact of concrete childhood experiences, and hence of intrafamilial violence, as an etiological factor in psychopathology.

Along with these two main reasons, we can also emphasize the dissatisfaction of the clinical psychologist, who, when confronted with abuse situations, fails to grasp not only their present complexity but also the process of their evolution in time.

This, as we have said, does not signify a lack of studies on the single or multiple factors contributing to family violence or the short- and long-term effects on the victim. In this regard, we can cite the large and complex ecological model proposed in 1980 by J. Garbarino and reported by Browne (1988). This work omits neither the predisposing individual, familial, social, and cultural factors, nor the mediation factors represented by the network of support and social assistance, nor the causative factors such as the events of everyday life, the family members' interpretations and perceptions of these events and of their stress potential (Figure 1).

Likewise, we have no shortage of in-depth research into more specific aspects of this problem, such as the behavioral, emotional, and cognitive impact of violence on children.

Brown (1984), for instance, shows that tendencies toward delinquent behavior are linked to experiences of childhood neglect rather than physical battering. Oates, Forrest, and Peacock (1985) point out that the childhood victims of violence have personalities characterized by low self-esteem, insecurity, and difficulties in relating to their peers. The studies on such children concur in highlighting depressive tendencies, passivity, inhibitedness, anxiety, dependence,

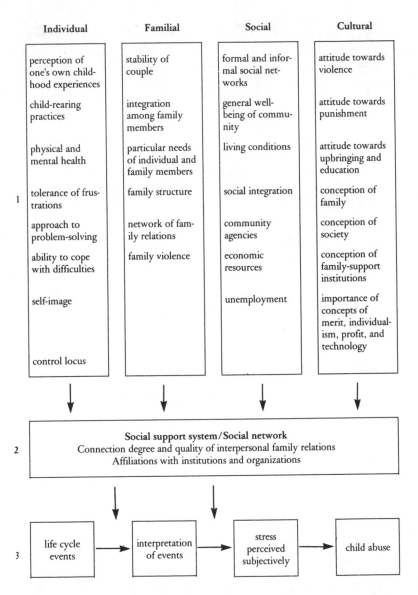

FIGURE 1: The ecological model of child abuse: 1. predisposing factors; 2. mediation of factors; 3. precipitating factors (modified by J. Garbarino, reported by Browne, 1988, p. 46).

rage, and aggressivity (Gaensbauer & Sands, 1979; Martin & Rode-heffer, 1980). More systematic research has accentuated specific be-havior patterns in abused children, who exhibit successive or com-bined sequences of "approach" and "avoidance" in social contacts (George & Main, 1979). Or else these investigations underscore the propensity in abused children for assailing or threatening the adult with typical kinds of aggressive behavior known as "molestation" (Bowlby, 1984).

Another course of inquiry has focused on the personal characteris-tics of abusive parents, especially the mother-child relationship. Now and then, researchers have portrayed depressive tendencies, depen-dence needs, social isolation, and fear of separation from the mother as explanatory or predisposing factors in regard to manifestations of violence toward children (Morris & Gould, 1963; Seel & Pollock, 1968).

We cannot help noting that, in our eyes, both of these lines of investigation, whether concentrating on children or on parents, show the limits of an approach that tends to favor the characteristics of the individual and ignore an overall understanding of the abusive family. Nevertheless, we believe that several insights gained by De Lozier (1982) can be of some interest if they are reframed and interpreted in the light of family norms. Indeed, De Lozier points out the presence of the abusive mother's "anxious preoccupation" with the well-being of her own parents. The author emphasizes that in the abusive mother's childhood, she experienced a typical inversion of roles, which made her feel responsible for taking care of and protecting the adult.

These observations deserve to be developed and deepened. How and why do such past experiences continue to operate in the present? In what ways and under what circumstances are the relations with the family of origin connected to the specific abuse dynamic?

Family studies (Boszormenyi-Nagy & Spark, 1973; Masson, 1981; Minuchin, 1974) head in this direction. Masson in particular has demonstrated that neglect and abuse emerge in a family system in which the "parentification" of the children in the family of origin (first generation, grandparents) does not end with the marriages of the children; rather, the parentification survives actively, causing unsuitable parental conduct in the second generation. On the other hand, this insight would confirm the well-established opinion (Cicchetti & Rizley, 1981; Main & Goldwyn, 1984) that abuse is a repetitive phenomenon developing from one generation to the next, which is precisely the reason why it is important to stop this abused/abusing intergenerational cycle (Cirillo & Di Blasio, 1988).

Adopting the Game Metaphor

As we can see, the brief outline that we have sketched here reveals a sharp break between two diverse kinds of investigation. There are the researchers who home in on behavioral and personality traits both in the abusive parents and in the battered children; and there are the family theorists, who ferret out the rules and interactive modalities of the family group as a whole. It is very difficult to cover both the individual aspects and the group aspects of the familial dynamics, which may be a further reason—in this case, a conceptual one—for the slow progress in explaining the dynamics of abuse.

Then again, for several years now, family therapists have adhered to a system notion that operates in essentially holistic terms (Bertalanffy, 1968); this tendency has handicapped their analysis of the intrinsic significance of the responses of individuals. On the other hand, these responses by themselves are insufficient for thoroughly understanding a phenomenon as complex as abuse, which impedes the overall functioning of a family.

During the past few years, a new route has opened up, allowing us to escape that rigid family/individual dichotomy and hence the stasis of explanatory approaches. We are referring to the adoption of a model based on the "game metaphor" (Selvini Palazzoli et al., 1985, 1989). This method permits us to integrate the level of individual functioning with that of the determinants in the social environment, through the intermediate level of the relational patterns in the family group.

The concept of "family game" (taken on by the Selvini Palazzoli group with the meaning attached to it by Crozier & Friedberg, 1980) is applied to the way in which the relations among the family members are organized and evolve over time. The game metaphor, beyond the notion of system, enables us to integrate the individual level with the superindividual level as represented by both the familial functioning and the social functioning. This approach recognizes a relative autonomy of emotions, behaviors, and strategies in the individual family members, even if they are all closely integrated in the interactive organization that encompasses them. From this point of view, it is obvious that an individual plays a certain game because he has certain feelings, motives, and goals, but it is also true that he has certain feelings, motives, and goals because he is part of a collective game that influences him and limits the moves at his disposal (Selvini Palazzoli et al., 1989).

This multidimensional way of thinking represented our theoretical anchor as we refine our practical treatment. These suppositions can orient us not only in diagnosing and treating families, but also in the more general technical procedures for gathering information during the referral phase, for making our first contact with the family, taking charge of the case, and organizing our relations with the other agencies. We begin observing the family game at the tragic moment when the problem of abuse is revealed; we then proceed gradually, during family contacts with the staff members, until the child enters the Residential Center and the diagnostic and therapeutic work is settled. Our observations of the family game offer a path that strikes us as illuminating and productive, both for grasping the complexity of the abuse phenomenon and for working out suitable ways of tackling it in the various phases of the process.

The chapters that follow are devoted to illustrating how these assumptions can lead to a concrete proposal for diagnostic and therapeutic work.

II | IS "TREATMENT" POSSIBLE FOR THE PATIENT WHO DOES NOT REQUEST IT?

Mandated Therapy: A Gamble

In 1980, ONE OF US (SC) was invited to join the group that would make up the team of the future CAF, the Help Center for Abused Children and Families in Crisis. Unfortunately, he did not have the foggiest notion about the problem of child abuse—even though he had spent years working as a psychologist in juvenile institutions and consultation and had completed training in family therapy. This absolute ignorance was, we believe, common among many therapists of that period and even among our future CAF colleagues. In approaching the problem, we relied almost exclusively on North American material, for example, pragmatic textbooks and educational films aimed at supplying a background in child abuse and instruction for the professionals who had to deal with it. As we look back after so many years, we do not recall that any of this abundant documentation explicitly discussed what we initially saw as an enormous contradiction between therapy and coercion. Even Kempe's small manual (Kempe & Kempe, 1978), taking for granted the necessity of treating a family that abuses its children, merely lists several useful tricks for overcoming the reluctance of abusive parents to get involved in a treatment program.

On the other hand, we vividly recall the basic objection that was

16

raised when our first project (worked out on paper after our formative training and our subsequent reflections)[1] was accepted by the
scientific committee and by the assembly of CAF members: "How
can you hope to treat a person who has not asked you for any sort
of help and who comes only at the orders of Juvenile Court? The
basic prerequisite for therapy—namely, spontaneous motivation—
has fallen by the wayside!"

Since at that time we had not yet come face to face with even a
single abusive family, we lacked any counterarguments to that objection, which we somewhat shared, although without admitting it.
That was why our decision to venture out on the road of mandated
therapy was unanimously labeled "a gamble."

Now, after eight years of hard but enthralling work, we feel we
can clarify the dynamics of this gamble more intelligently and describe our first results.

Why the Abusive Family Does Not Seek Help

At the outset of our work, the "gamble" of nonvoluntary therapy
struck us as a third possibility, beyond the alternative of either crimi-
nalizing the abusive parents or remaining indifferent to abused children.

As we have said, we realized that, while our American colleagues
may have failed to notice it, the expression "nonvoluntary therapy"
sounds like a contradiction in terms within the field of Italian psychology. Therapists have always emphasized that any therapy presupposes a request for help and an underlying motivation; the latter is
virtually the dynamo that can galvanize the patient's desire to change,
aiding him in overcoming any sort of inertia or resistance.

If, on the other hand, she is coerced into therapy, a recalcitrant
individual will submit to and endure a procedure that she has not

---

1. The draft for the operational model of the Center was done by Stefano Cirillo
together with Bruna Bianchi and Marinella Malacrea (who then helped him form
the therapeutic staff) as well as Ernesto Caffo, a member of CAF's first board of
directors and Secretary of the Italian Association for the Prevention of Child Abuse,
which had been established a short time earlier.

chosen, and that she may find distasteful, unwelcome, or even in-comprehensible. Since her chief goal in entering therapy is to avoid a greater evil, she feels no genuine impulse to change. Nevertheless, we believe that one can transcend this blatant contradiction by chal-lenging the assumption that the lack of a request for help always automatically betokens a lack of motivation for change.

When an adult abuses his own child, the very nature of the problem makes it extremely difficult, perhaps impossible, for him to seek help outside his family, even if he is willing to extricate himself from his predicament. In fact, the abusive parent knows very well that owning up to his conduct is equivalent to denouncing himself: he has violated not only a deep-rooted social taboo but also a legally sanctioned behavioral norm. Far more than the person who admits to having a symptom that social custom views as culpable or shame-ful (say, alcoholism or, until recently, homosexuality), the parent who confesses to abusing his own children realizes that he may expose himself not only to censure and disapproval, but also to the risk of a criminal trial. These factors militate against his openly seeking help.

It would indeed be absurd to expect abusive parents to be so farsighted, to have such utter trust in the judiciary and the social health services that they will turn themselves in as child abusers and suffer the consequences. These parents would scarcely choose to face certain penalties today for the sake of uncertain help tomorrow. Indeed, beyond the so-called law for repentants—an exceptional mea-sure, devised for an entirely different type of criminal situation—the Italian legal system provides no concrete incentives for the confessed criminal who intends to cooperate in his own rehabilitation. Never-theless, something has happened along these lines in the area of drug dependency. Law no. 663 of 1986 allows the placement of a sub-stance abuser in a hospice with a therapeutic and rehabilitative pro-gram as an alternative to prison. This applies even if the addict has committed a crime (for instance, robbery), whereas, earlier such a criminal was not allowed to benefit from this period of probation with the social service. In our specific area, a radical innovation could be introduced by the Russo Jervolino-Vassalli bill concerning the penal custody of minors (4 February 1988). Article 12 of this bill — noteworthy within the context of the new trial code — permits a suspension of trial for a parent charged with crimes against a minor child. The goal of this measure is to provide a possibility of restoring the family relationship.

The diverse legal system certainly accounts, at least in part, for the indifference that North American researchers have always shown toward the problem of mandated therapy. After all, in their milieu, it is unquestioningly accepted that an external incentive can trigger an actual change as much as an autonomous motivation (which, moreover, we must always simply infer!)[2]

It seems legitimate to suppose that at least some abusive parents fervently wish to modify their own state of suffering, which is both the cause and the effect of abuse. And presumably, their desire to change is no more and no less intense than that of other people who experience different sorts of problems and disturbances within their own families (psychiatric symptoms, drug dependency, serious conflicts, etc.), but who find it almost impossible to seek help.

Thus, in regard to a family caught in a tragic web of bad relationships, it would be extremely unfair for the social system (or institutions) to limit itself to merely punishing socially aberrant behavior rather than offering some kind of help, an opportunity to move toward a better arrangement (Cirillo, 1986a).

Sociofamilial Factors in the Absence of a Request for Help

The avoidance of self-incrimination as an obstacle to seeking help is common in most families with parents who abuse or neglect their children. This reluctance leads to a characteristic pattern of responses

---

2. Even Unité, headed by Odette Masson, benefits from the existence of the Swiss Service de la protection de la jeunesse (Service for the Protection of Youth), in an institutional framework that is significantly different from ours.

from parents accused of mistreatment. Almost without exception, they strenuously—indeed unequivocally—deny any guilt; they come out with the most absurd pretexts and justifications; they throw up a wall of obstinate reticence, impervious silence; they try to blame someone else—a small child, a teacher, even the family cat!

Distrust in the social health services and their potential for providing genuine help can be triggered by particular sociocultural contexts. This is the case with lower-class families, immigrants, or members of ethnic minorities, who have a history of dealing with public welfare on the basis of the authority's hypocrisy and exploitation of the economic resources of the social services (Malagoli Togliatti & Rocchetta Tofani, 1987). In these situations, the caseworkers are often resigned to distributing non-goal-oriented financial help instead of attempting to intervene with an all-encompassing plan.

Moreover, people in the deprived cultural strata are unaware of psychotherapy as a resource (whereas now, in the middle-class milieu, it has become a fad, even a status symbol). The notion that one can tackle and solve a problem through verbal communication is culturally foreign to the underprivileged.

Aside from these general aspects, the specific family dynamics of an individual case may impede any request for help.

Take the example of nine-year-old Alex. He was referred to the social services by his school physician, who had repeatedly noticed that the boy had bruises caused by blows. Alex was the eldest child of a couple who ran a small business together with the father's parents. Alex had been referred by his teacher at the end of his first year of school for psychomotor instability and for being unable to follow scholastic rules. The parents, summoned by the school doctor, had agreed to a psychological consultation at the Children's Mental Health Service. But they had ignored the doctor's advice, even though Alex's behavior had eventually worsened. Despite his teacher's insistence, the parents had done nothing to help their son, who was then left back in third grade.

How are we to explain this attitude in people of average education, who, even if suspicious of public agencies, were economically able to pay for private consultation?

Alex's parents, Franco and Maria, were very young—22 and 20—when they married; they had to get married because Maria was expecting a baby. The young couple moved into a tiny apartment in the large building owned by Franco's family; the apartment was located above the workshop which was the headquarters of the small family business. Maria put up with this situation very reluctantly; she was unhappy because her own parents had done nothing to help her out, thus forcing her to accept the help of her in-laws, who, she felt, dominated Franco. Inexperienced and unhappy, she acted irritably toward little Alex from the start; she soon preferred leaving him with his grandmother, thereby managing to escape into her own work for a while. When Alex turned four, Maria decided to have a second child, hoping that a larger family would compel Franco to approach his parents about an independent apartment for the couple and their children. They got their apartment, and Maria quit her job in order to devote herself to their second child, Simonetta. Alex was looked after by his grandparents for a period of several months, after which he returned to his family and his mother's care. As could be predicted, he was naughty and demanding, jealous of his little sister—he missed his grandmother's attentiveness and was hostile to his mother's impatient demands.

Nevertheless, the mother-son couple would probably have managed to overcome their initial difficulties and achieve some harmony, had it not been for Franco, who exploited the boy's discontent as an outlet for his own anger toward Maria. He was fed up with recriminations from his wife, who kept reproaching him for his subjugation to his parents. In the evening, whenever he came home from work, he would find her engrossed in long telephone calls with her mother, who lived several miles away; Maria was pouring out her bitterness about her marriage. As a result, whenever Maria scolded Alex and asked Franco to step in, the father would side with the boy and accuse his wife of treating Alex coldly, of not knowing how to handle him (unlike his grandmother), and of favoring their daughter. In this way, Franco unwittingly reinforced Alex's hostility toward his mother, instigating the boy against her and making him even more rebellious and harder to discipline.[3]

During this phase of family life, Alex began attending school, and here it was suggested that he be sent for psychological consultation. Franco, quite understandably, was reluctant to accept this advice. He was convinced that "there is nothing wrong with the boy." His wife, he felt, should act differently toward their son (and, above all, toward Franco himself, even if this wish was not explicitly voiced). It is more difficult to understand Maria's resistance to taking her son to the Children's Mental Health Service. There are well-known cases in which a mother is quick to call her offspring "abnormal," thereby hoping to pass the buck when her husband accuses her of not raising the child properly. Why didn't Maria seize this opportunity? Perhaps because, just like her spouse, she felt disappointed and frustrated by their marital life and, like him, she sought comfort in her family of origin. Of course, this represents only half the vicious circle; the other half is the fact that an unresolved bond with one's family of origin may cause an inadequate investment in, and therefore maladjustment to, one's own marriage.

But while Franco, as an only child, could count on indiscriminate parental support, Maria, profoundly jealous of Franco's secure bond with his own family, felt she got little support from her mother, a recent widow, who had moved in with her son in order to look after his children. This was why Maria constantly chose the strategy of overwhelming her mother with

---

3. For an exhaustive treatment of the phenomenon of instigation, see Selvini Palazzoli et al. (1989, pp. 95–132).

her complaints about Franco and Alex: Maria was secretly hoping to make her mother feel guilty and to induce her to think more about her daughter, be concerned about her, commiserate with her. Maria was thus not really motivated to do anything about her son's problem, since she, like Franco, hoped to benefit from it.

This did not mean that Alex's behavior was not growing more and more intolerable for her, inasmuch as the boy, strengthened by his father's support, kept acting worse and worse. The father's support, mind you, was purely exploitive: Franco never really spent that much time with the boy or showered that much affection on him in order to make up for Maria's harshness. He was absorbed in his work, and during the rare moments that he spent with his wife and children, he limited himself simply to being permissive with Alex—in contrast with Maria's way of raising the child. Whenever an exasperated Maria lost control and hit the boy hard, she had no interest in admitting that she had done so because of the exasperation that Alex had triggered in her. She was certain that this would only arouse her husband's disapproval. Franco, although suspecting the abuse, connived at hushing it up, because he did not know how his parents might react (toward him too) and because he feared social censure and legal repercussions. Furthermore, Maria knew that if she owned up to abusing her son, she would lose all hope of sympathy from her mother, who would be horrified by her daughter's conduct and unremitting in condemning her. Thus, just as three years earlier Alex's parents had refused to take him to a psychologist, they would now emphatically refuse to admit that the boy was being abused and that both he and they were in urgent need of help.

As we shall see later on, only a notification of the judicial authorities can lead to an intervention guaranteeing, first and foremost, a child's physical and mental safety and providing a basis for attempts to salvage the family unit.

Several Exceptions: When the Family
Presents Itself Spontaneously

During the past few years, we have sometimes encountered what seemed like exceptions to the rule: cases in which families reported abuse spontaneously.

Contrary to what people might think (or what we used to think), these cases are a lot trickier than the ones assigned to us by Juvenile Court.

In one group of "spontaneous" cases, it is a relative—a member of the extended family or the spouse—who reports the abusive parent. Here, the caseworkers have to deal with a family that has already internally identified the "villain" to be punished (rather than, and prior to, being treated). The person who reports the abuser thereby presents herself as the "good guy," ignoring that fact that, as a family member, she has contributed to the type of familial interaction that has led to the abuse for which the "bad guy" is responsible.

At this point, when a family member asks for help, the professional must exhibit the skill of a tightrope walker in taking the necessary steps to protect the minors while simultaneously avoiding any confirmation of the splitting of the family into "bad guys" and "good guys." Such an endorsement would make any therapeutic efforts impossible. Indeed, the informer implicitly tries to present herself as a "colleague," who is exclusively concerned with the welfare of the children and completely outside any dynamics linked to their abuse. If the professional accepts this self-portrayal as bare fact, he ultimately reinforces the dysfunctional family modality that has led one of the members to take on the abusive role. Such an error on the therapist's part is difficult to correct.[4] Let us look at an example.

Mr. D'Andrea (as we will call him) turned up at our social worker's office without an appointment. He requested help for his nine-year-old daughter Ines: Her mother, who had been

---

4. In regard to this irreparable mistake, see Selvini Palazzoli (1984).

treated for depression for some time, beat her violently because the girl was slow when eating and when doing her chores. The father, a salesman, tried to be home by the time his daughter returned from her after-school group, which she attended so that she might eat at least one meal away from her mother. But sometimes, the father was forced to stay out much longer, and at such moments he feared for his daughter's safety.

Our social worker instantly telephoned Mrs. D'Andrea in the husband's presence. She repeated to the mother every detail of the man's story while making sure that she didn't take sides with or against his version. The social worker offered to meet with both parents together several days later, and she then discussed the father. By failing to inform Mrs. D'Andrea about what she had learned from her husband, the social worker would have established an alliance with him against the wife. She would have signaled her unconditional acceptance of his story and treated the mother with the caution reserved for a person who is considered unbalanced or unworthy of trust.

Subsequent work with the family showed that Mr. D'Andrea had married a woman who aroused his feelings of protectiveness because she was on bad terms with her family. However, when his daughter was born shortly after the wedding, he had rapidly shifted his affection from the mother to the child. The more hostilely his jealous wife behaved toward this close father-daughter rapport, the more attentive the husband acted toward the little girl. He wanted to make up to her for her mother's coldness, which he blamed on the bad relationship that his wife had had with her own mother during her childhood. In this way, the vicious circle fed on itself, eventually leading to abuse; and obviously, when the father sought help at our Center, his move, rather than upsetting the game, reinforced it. It was only the caseworker's rigorous efforts to maintain absolute neutrality during the phase of receiving the report that prevented our intervention from ultimately becoming pathogenic. Thanks to her neutral stance, the family therapy proceeded correctly, leading to remedies for both the abuse and the wife's depression.

Nevertheless, it must be said that in this category of cases, in which the informer is related to the abuser, a skilled professional instantly knows that a trap is opening before him, even if he doesn't always know how to sidestep it.[5] By contrast, he has a far more difficult time extricating himself in a second group of cases, which occur, however, much more infrequently in our experience.

In this situation, the abuser turns himself in. The first few of these cases that we encountered were solved in an extremely frustrating way, even though we approached them somewhat arrogantly, convinced as we were that they resembled cases of spontaneous therapy. In hindsight, we realized that self-denunciation was a message sent to another family member, usually the spouse: "I've done so much for our child, a lot more than you have. If you don't reciprocate by doing something for me, I'm going to beat the hell out of the child, I just can't help it."[6]

Among these cases in which the abuser turned himself in, there were two families in particular; both included a parent who was "devoted to home and family" (the abuser seeking help), and a parent who ignored the daily obligations. In one case, the husband had deserted his wife and two small children; in the other, the wife, citing her own job responsibilities, waved off the husband's appeals for affection, which she perceived as stifling.

In both these cases, the therapy for the abuse brought back the disengaged spouse somewhat, but not enough to fulfill the other spouse's needs; thus, the results were only partial in regard to the latter's behavior toward the children.

While the abuse ended in both cases, it was replaced by an attitude of indifference toward the children, who were handed over to an

---

5. For now, we will not go into the request often made by the informer to keep his actions a secret; this is part of the more general problem of confidentiality in family therapy (Selvini Palazzoli & Prata, 1981).

6. In regard to a request for help as the ultimate move in a game, see Selvini (1988, pp. 210–211).

institution. Today, we would interpret such an institutionalization of children as a hostile and vindictive message to the spouse: "If you won't do anything for me, then don't imagine I'm willing to sacrifice myself anymore for *your* children." A failure to decipher in time the true relational meaning of abuse has prevented therapists from attaining results that are within their reach.

It ought to be observed that, in such cases, the abuser regards the offspring purely as a means of imprisonment by the spouse—that is, the abusive parent feels that, if it weren't for the children, he or she would be free to get away. The parent sees them not as persons with whom to work out a relationship, but as fetters that the spouse skillfully uses to chain the abusive parent to "everyday life"—fetters that have to be avoided. Thus, the abuser focuses solely on the spouse and his/her disagreement—that is the game; and the abuser does this so thoroughly that he or she views the children purely as emissaries of his or her abuse and therefore *unworthy of respect*—hired assassins, who deserve nothing but beatings. This crude logic is frequent and tragic, and its ultimate and natural epilogue is to place the child in an institution.

The Pitfalls of the Spontaneous Context

Beyond this mistake in deciphering the abusive conduct, all the cases described in the preceding paragraph contain a more serious contextual error, which we kept repeating for a long time when dealing with spontaneous requests for help.

If a parent consults a psychologist about the problems of her child or asks for marital counseling to solve conflicts that cause the child to suffer, she is triggering an action of intervention for the good of the minor. On the other hand, if a family member reports child abuse inflicted within his family by the informer or a relative, he is implicitly revealing his inability to protect the child. For this reason, immediate intervention is necessary to protect the minor and stop the mistreatment until some other kind of action, say psychotherapy, can remove the causes.

The assumption of this difference is a fundamental task for the professional who learns about a case of actual or potential child abuse. It is her first duty to immediately report the situation to the court—something that did not occur in the cases described above. It then becomes the job of the Juvenile Court judge to decide whether any measures should be taken to protect the minor (for instance, his removal from the abuser), just as it is the job of the regular judge to verify if there are any grounds for legal action against the abuser.

It is obvious that this initiative is extremely delicate, and the caseworkers can start out reluctantly, their attitude contrasting with the way the professionals in the psychosocial and health areas may view their roles. Since those professionals see themselves exclusively as providing help, they feel repugnance toward an action of social control such as notifying the police or the court.

Such a decision is even more difficult to carry out as a response to a spontaneous request for help made by the abuser himself or by a member of his family. In such an instance, the caseworker fears being thought of as a spy by the person seeking help (or regards herself as one), and she therefore puts off the thankless step as long as possible. Nevertheless, our subsequent experiences with similar situations have reassured us that, after the initial moment of natural hostility, the client realizes that the caseworker, who is legally obligated to inform the court about the minor's condition, cannot shirk her duty. If the rules of the game are clear, people accept them: While no one may enjoy being fined or arrested by a policeman or sentenced by a judge, everyone understands that these people are simply complying with the codified norms of civil life. (At best, the perpetrator can try to soften up the policeman, escape him, or bribe the judge—moves that are provided for in the game of social roles!)

The client would react very differently if our professional, at the outset, marked the context[7] of his relationship to that person as exclusively a context of help, following all the proper rules of the private professional context, according to the formula: "You are spontaneously asking for my professional services because you trust

7. In regard to context markers and their rules, see Selvini Palazzoli (1970).

me, I agree to help you and I render my services to your satisfaction. Each of us has the right to cancel our contract at any time he likes." These aspects are not absolutely valid in the context that we are examining. If the spontaneous request for help is fulfilled by the caseworker, who succeeds in changing the situation, as in the above case of little Ines D'Andrea, then everything is fine. But suppose the opposite happens?

If the professional's efforts are fruitless and no change occurs, if the abuser fails to show up for appointments, if the clients fail to cooperate, or if the abuse goes on—for whatever reasons—what does the professional do? Faced with the persistence of harm or danger to the child and with the parent's absence, the therapist has no choice: He must, belatedly, notify the court about the situation. But at this point, the client will, quite justifiably, feel betrayed; for it was not originally made clear to her that her relationship with the professional belonged to a context of both help and monitoring—that is, the context of protection for the child.

Thus, at this point in the relationship, we can foresee violent protest reactions on the part of the client. These are not the conventional threats sometimes hurled at the professional when the latter immediately explains that he is legally bound to protect the minor; rather, these violent reactions are credible and genuine threats that, in a limited number of instances, can even turn into physical aggression against the imprudent therapist.

A not so negligible element comes into play if people operate within an unclearly marked context: the anxiety afflicting the professional whenever she witnesses the inexorable deterioration of her own intervention with the abusive family while the minor remains unprotected, exposed to an inherent danger of further abuse. When we began working, our team learned a basic lesson from Odette Masson's Lausanne team: "The first thing you do is establish secure conditions." This means making certain that you have fulfilled your obligations in regard to all the child-protection authorities (represented by the court and the social services), and that you have, above all, provided for the child's protection. It is only on this foundation that one can then try to erect a bold edifice for evaluating the family crisis and perhaps achieving a recovery.

False "Spontaneous Cases": When the Problem Lies with the Referring Person

During the past few years, another group of families came to us without being sent by the Juvenile Court; these families "spontaneously" requested help in regard to episodes of child abuse.

However, such confession does not originate within the perpetrator's family—unlike the two types of situations described above. These abusing families may turn themselves in because of a distorted relationship with the social health agencies. By and large, these are families that have been helped and followed up on for a long time, usually for a number of simultaneous reasons: economic difficulties, poor housing, unemployment, various pathologies such as alcoholism, disabilities, etc. When an episode of child abuse occurs in such a family, or, more frequently, a more serious episode follows others that the caseworkers chose to ignore, the social services are faced with the frustrating necessity of admitting defeat in regard to their own assistance efforts. However, rather than abandoning their roles of helping and supporting the family, they prefer to delay notifying the court; instead, they send the clients to another agency—in this particular case, to us. By so doing, they are simply hinting that the abuse will not be reported to the court so long as the family members agree to accept help in solving their not clearly identified problems.

At this point, of course, the family is formally invited to the specialized center and then contacts it more or less punctually. However, the family members tend to minimize the scope of the problems and to distort their nature. The parents, for instance, state that they have been advised to consult the agency in order to obtain information on how to cope with their "overactive" child or in order to solve marital conflicts, which have, however, already been "dealt with." They relegate their problems to an earlier period, when the husband drank or their housing was inadequate; but now, they conclude, "everything is fine." The professionals are thus faced with the paradoxical situation of having to address a "spontaneous" request for help even though the clients declare that they have no need of help. As a result, the caseworkers feel totally incapable of treating the pain that they nevertheless can sense beyond the smoke screen of lies, and they will be forced to endure being rapidly abandoned by the clients.

When the client refuses treatment, one can notify the referring agency; but this does not help us out of the impasse. We are stuck because the agency has failed to make the issue clear to the family in question: namely, that it will delay reporting the matter to the court (and thereby become a de facto accomplice), provided the family members enter a treatment program in regard to objectively verified abuse. When the family walks out on the treatment, it is even more difficult for the referral agency to notify the authorities belatedly. Time has passed, the memory of abuse has faded, the facts have been reshuffled too often. The family reports that it has gone to the center once or twice and received a great deal of help: "We have no more problems." And the referral agency is disarmed.

Notifying the Authorities: The Sole Instrument for Reaching the Family

It eventually dawned on us that the social health agencies' practice of sending us "false spontaneous cases" was not only unproductive but downright harmful. We came to realize this only after repeated experiences in which we ourselves had initiated this type of referral from the social services. At that time we were convinced that we would do better to work with families that, at least to some extent, "agreed" to enlist our help (an agreement that then proved to be a mere ritual). We must, nonetheless, admit that this kind of approach originates in a deep-seated tradition, which views Juvenile Court as "the last resort": If families are definitely shattered, the professionals have to notify the court, who will remove children from untreatable parents. This measure was regarded as a clinical disaster, precluding any further contact between the professional and the family, beyond pure and simple monitoring; consequently, the professional had to avoid seeing the family unless he glimpsed a possibility of offering "real" help.

In an earlier work (Azzoni, Cirillo, Di Blasio, et al., 1985), we described the change that we proposed for this traditional aspect of the relationship between the social services and Juvenile Court: We should go to the judge whenever we believe that the family in question is still capable of evolving but cannot be induced to undergo therapy.[8]

In these terms, notifying the court is not merely a responsible act on the part of the agency, which knows that its first duty is to protect the child. Involving the court is also a *clinical* instrument for communicating with a family that cannot be reached in any other way (Vassalli, 1987).

When parents send a child covered with bruises or bites to school, they are allowing the problem of violence to leave the family circle. They may be anxious (understandably so, for the reasons explained above) to deny the blatant evidence of their actions, and they may resort to ridiculous lies. Yet by enabling the teacher or the school doctor to literally touch the dismal effects of their unresolved problems, they are asking for help, albeit in a contradictory and distorted way. It is only by holding the parents to their responsibilities that we can help them escape from what strikes them as a hopeless dilemma. The first step to be taken is the immediate removal of the endangered child. However—and this must be clearly explained to the parents—such a precaution, while aimed chiefly at protecting the child, has a second and closely connected goal: The agency must investigate the possibilities of eliminating the root causes of the abuse and thereby restoring the positive child/parent relationship that is fundamental to the development of the child.

8. In our conception of taking recourse in Juvenile Court as one more therapeutic instrument, we are reassured by several authoritative interventions by judges. See, for instance, Moro (1988).

Naturally, the efforts of the professionals will be credible if they themselves are convinced. Why then don't they ask the judge to order the removal of all children suffering from a psychosis or other serious mental disturbances? Because even if the professionals feel that these symptoms are linked to a profound distortion of the interfamilial relations, they cannot necessarily place the ultimate blame on harmful actions committed by the parents. An abusive situation involves a patent harmful act, which calls for the protection of the child. But the professional knows that the underlying situation is similar to that of a psychosis, due to the presence of relational dysfunctions, which he hopes to tackle partly by notifying the court.[9]

9. On this topic, there is an interesting debate published in *Family Therapy Networker* (1985, vol. 9) on the distinction between victims and victimizers in cases of spousal violence. A feminist approach (*Family Therapy Networker*, 1985, pp. 9–11) ferociously criticized several of Minuchin's statements (published in the preceding issue) about the difficulties in discriminating between victim and victimizer in cases of domestic violence. The writers, forcefully employing the tools of common sense about obvious physical injuries (black eyes, broken bones, skin burns, coagulated blood) cited the gap in physical strength between men and women. On these grounds, they flatly rejected any use of the systemic theory that could impugn such evidence. A sound compromise was offered (*Family Therapy Networker*, 1985, vol. 9, no. 4, p. 4) that we feel clears up the apparent contradiction between the two extremes: "Battered women are responsible for the violence they suffer" and "Family therapists who adhere to this viewpoint are insensitive and antifeminist." The author of the letter, who tried to safeguard the foundations of the family therapist's "neutrality" while simultaneously emphasizing that violence against women is unacceptable in a civilized society, demonstrated that the question was epistemologically misstated. The language of "crime and victim" is legalese, and, on a legal plane, the man who beats his wife is guilty of a crime and must be punished. However, the field of therapy is not concerned with right or wrong, guilt or innocence; its goal is to modify behavior. How then can we help a couple if we do not understand the specific dynamics that generate the interdependence of abuser and abused?

III | TAKING ON CASES IN MANDATED SITUATIONS

The Contextual Prerequisites

IN CHAPTERS I AND II, we tried to convey the emotional climate surrounding the emergence of the Center and our first experiences in working with abuse situations; we also attempted to reconstruct the beginnings of our Center, its difficulties and obstacles, its trials and errors.

Now we would like to take a step forward and present the current procedures we use in our psychological work with an abusive family. Our experiences suggest that these procedures are useful and satisfying, at least on a practical level; still, we have every hope of improving and perfecting them in the future.

Before commencing our therapeutic work with a family, we feel that we have to establish certain preconditions by carrying out a sequence of operations within the overall process of our taking on a case. If these preconditions are lacking, then any psychological intervention is quite likely to fail, just as any errors and omissions during the process of taking on a case are hard to make up for in later phases. We will now have a look at the chief contextual elements that, according to our experience, constitute the prerequisites for subsequent clinical work.

The Report and the Relationship between
the Referring Agencies

As is all too obvious, the entire process of referral is triggered by a suspicion that a child is the victim of violence within his family. This suspicion becomes a certainty in the frequent cases in which the observer notes unmistakable signs of blows, bruises, scratches, hematomas, or else neglected or inadequate clothing, malnutrition, serious medical and/or hygienic deficiencies, and even sexual abuse that is explicitly and convincingly revealed by the victim—for instance, to a friend or a teacher.

Too often, however, even with such blatant evidence, professionals assume that they can solve a problem through informal and indirect procedures—for example, by summoning the family on a false pretext, imposing a mock-friendly chat, trying to gain the trust and confidence of the parents, obtaining assistance for the family's most immediate and concrete economic problems, and so on.

In other instances, however, the caseworker assumes that he can tackle this kind of situation by involving an authority figure—say, the school principal or a teacher—in order to investigate the causes of the injuries or neglect and by paternalistically urging the parents to take better care of their children. These efforts, as caseworkers know from experience, are futile, or else, at best, produce a short-lived change.[1] After several weeks or months, the child once again displays signs of violence or neglect. As for incest, a belittling of the problem can lead to even more serious consequences for the victim, who, realizing that she is neither believed nor protected, may react by committing self-aggression, running away, attempting suicide, using drugs, etc.

Caseworkers in schools, health agencies, or welfare services should never forget that in their capacity as public officials they are legally

---

1. We must note that, as a rule, the parent responding to the therapist's invitation is not the abuser, he or she is the silent accomplice of a more clearly violent partner. As such, the responding parent participates in a violent dynamic that he or she cannot or will not modify.

obligated to notify the judicial authorities about any offense involving child abuse on the basis of articles 330 and 333 of the Italian
Civil Code and any crimes which can be prosecuted without the
need of the victim's complaint on the basis of articles 570, 571, and
572 of the Penal Code (Ichino Pellizzi, 1988).

Granted, it may not be easy to take such measures, especially
when one is persuaded that the abuse is symptomatic of a disturbance
that ought to be treated rather than punished. Yet it is equally true
that the failure to act on these obligations signals two factors: a
widespread tendency to downplay and nullify the necessary rights of
minors and the conviction that an abusive and violent family does
less damage than the social services, the police, or the court system.
Nevertheless, we know that the short- and long-term effects on the
mental health of battered victims are extremely serious—indeed, far
more so than the specialized psychological and psychiatric literature
assumed until just a few years ago.[2]

We must therefore come up with operative procedures that, as
we have said, transcend the current situation, in which either the
perpetrator is incriminated or the problem is denied and the victim
is left feeling helpless.

When we are confronted with cases of family violence, our first
objective—and we never tire of repeating it—is to protect the minors.
This is possible only if the professionals take advantage of the available
resources and get directly involved rather than ignoring their obligation
to investigate, inform, report—hence, to notify the authorities.

The first step consists of gathering reliable evidence of the abuse

---

2. The literature on short-term and long-term consequences of violence has revealed
the presence of disturbances in various functions and various spheres of the child's
life—for instance: learning; the expression of aggression; the ability to socialize, and,
more generally, to structure interpersonal bonds; and even the development of his
intelligence and linguistic capacity. For more details, the reader can consult several
works on this topic: Allen & Oliver, 1982; Bagley & McDonald, 1984; Barahal,
Waterman, & Martin, 1981; Bolton, Reich, & Gutierres, 1977; Bowman, Blix, &
Coons, 1985; Brassard, Germain, & Hart, 1987; Deschamps, Pavageau, Pierson, &
Deschamps, 1982; Elmer, 1978; Friedrich, Einbender, & Luecke, 1983; Monane,
Leichter, & Lewis, 1984; Pardeck, 1988; Post, 1982, Sack & Dale, 1982; Shengold,
1985; Toro, 1982; Byrne & Valdiserri, 1982.

as quickly as possible. A teacher can, for instance, draw up a detailed report on the basis of her own observations; she can have the child examined by the school doctor in order to gauge the actual magnitude of the physical injuries and, if possible, their causes. She can request help from the agencies that deal with suspicious cases; but she should not fully turn the problem over to them. By passing the buck, she would be shirking her duty to file a report or inform the appropriate authorities, in the false hope that others will assume her responsibilities. It is only thanks to notifications accompanied by medical reports and by detailed and complete descriptions that we can obtain timely protection for the minors through the courts, whose actions also leave room for a possible recovery of the family. All too often, the caseworker who sidesteps these obligations will ultimately sentence the children and their families to the prison of chronic violence (Cirillo, 1986a). In the absence of clear and timely legal measures, a caseworker, although an expert in social and psychological problems, will find himself coping with reticent families who are unwilling to accept any help.

In such cases, support and psychological treatment constitute resources, possibilities, usable opportunities only after a judicial mechanism is activated.

It is obvious that the integration of these two aspects is indispensable and not to be ignored. This is the sole basis on which the notification of the court can operate as a tool with a great clinical potential, as we indicated in the previous chapter.

The Juvenile Court Order and Temporary Measures

The process of notifying Juvenile Court[3] offers, at least in our experience, an accessible, effective, and preferable route, precisely because, along with protecting the child, it sets into motion the psychological

---

3. In regard to abuse, the Italian legal system provides for two types of interventions. Once charges are filed, the Criminal Court applies penal sanctions to the abuser; on the other hand, Juvenile Court has the job of shielding and protecting minor victims of violence. However, these two approaches cannot always be integrated. Indeed, Italian legislation does not oblige the Criminal Court to notify

work with the family. Juvenile Court judges have always struck us as eager to view the minor's return to her family as being in her best interest once the family is capable of adequately performing its child-rearing functions (Bertotti & Malacrea, 1987).

In sifting the available evidence, Juvenile Court is, as a rule, concerned primarily with determining whether the charges are founded. The judge can therefore arrange for an initial investigation by the social services, which may, of course, in rare cases, fail to come up with the necessary proof. More often, their inquiry exposes serious and complex family situations. An imprecise and hesitant notification may cause social services to intervene belatedly and against notable resistance. In contrast, a thorough report including a medical and/or psychosocial profile will enable the court to adopt timely measures for protecting the child and launching a family evaluation program.

This phase of the process involves the psychosocial caseworkers, who have the job of ferreting out the reasons for the violence, evaluating the situation, and furnishing useful material for setting up definitive programs aimed at shielding the child.

The court order, together with the referral and the report supplied by the informers, is thus the second indispensable premise for building an effective diagnostic context. Obviously, in formulating the temporary order, the judge takes into account all the dangerous facets of the family situation. If a child is at great risk, the judge can demand his immediate removal from the family; in case of low risk, he can allow the minor to remain at home.

But either measure is, obviously, incomplete if the authorities are unwilling to intervene by providing support and evaluation as well as monitoring for both parents and children. It is clear that the

---

Juvenile Court, while the latter must notify the former. As a result, Juvenile Court may not be asked to get involved in a case. This fact indubitably reduces the possibility of adopting adequate programs for protecting minors. Hence, a huge number of cases are routed to Juvenile Court, "where the civil judge is officially obligated to ascertain (even without the victim's complicity) the various situations of abandonment or harm to a minor and perhaps, if the judge deems it necessary, to send the parents to Criminal Court" (Ichino Pellizzi, 1988, p. 39).

Juvenile Court cannot do an adequate job of protection without the help of the social services and caseworkers with a background in psychology; these caseworkers must specify the problems hampering a family and evaluate its ability to change. Otherwise, the judge would merely be acting as a rigid censor, who hands down decisions based essentially on general norms rather than on evaluation of concrete data (Vassalli, 1987).

On the other hand, any efforts by sociopsychological experts will be wasted if there is no disposition clearly signaling—to the family as well—the need to protect the child against inadequate parental behavior. What credibility and what chances of intervention would the psychologist or social worker have if the family were completely relieved of any legal responsibility? Absolutely none. In fact, the family would feel legitimately authorized to ignore the opinions of the social workers and to perpetuate the same relational dynamics that led to the child abuse in the first place.

Defining the Tasks of the Agencies and Their Cooperation

In formulating its order, the Juvenile Court requires measures that may seem punitive in the eyes of the family. For instance, the judge may have the child removed from his home, limit or suspend parental authority, and either name a guardian or assign the child to the social services. On the other hand, the judge also arranges for monitoring, support, and a diagnostic evaluation that can furnish material for a definitive program. The steps insuring the child's protection can thus be translated into coordinated operations of support and monitoring, for both the child and the family (Azzoni, Cirillo, Di Blasio, et al., 1985; Cirillo, Di Blasio, Malacrea, & Vassalli, 1990).

In complex situations like that of abuse, many specialized caseworkers with different tasks must cooperate in supplying the material for working out a definitive program. Among these professionals, however, there is an ever-present risk of conflicts and breaches dictated not only by an inability to reconcile diverse approaches and philosophies, but also by the intrinsically limited nature of each point of view. This second problem, which makes integration necessary is, in our opinion, certainly greater than the first.

The difficulties arise not only from uncritical adherence to one's own frame of reference (which can be medical, social, legal, psychological, etc.), but also from a tendency to draw general conclusions from partial observations. Take the example of the residential workers assigned to a child who, as a victim of violence, is removed from his family and placed in an institution. These residential workers will, logically, focus their attention on the minor, on her disorders, her psychological difficulties, her problems in relating to her parents. They may even succeed in producing significant changes in the child's scholastic performance and in her personal sphere. However, if parental visits upset the child and arouse her fears, the workers, upon noticing these reactions, may be led to regard the parents, and consequently their relationship to the child, as inadequate and untreatable.

A similar problem may arise with a social worker, who, in meeting the parents or visiting their home, has to evaluate, say, the living conditions rather than the mother's organizational skills or the father's ability to earn a living. The professional may conclude that the family's violence and crisis are rooted in the father's unemployment, the family's economic difficulties and social hardships, or certain critical events. As a result, the social worker may be induced to side with the family by putting it on welfare. In the same way, family psychotherapy, if not accompanied by judicial measures and interventions by the social services, could lead to the belief that comprehension and explanation of the difficulties, motivations, and expectations of the actors and of the reasons for the crisis might be enough to produce changes necessary to prevent the repetition of the violence. And finally, the judge, likewise, risks generalizing her own intervention when she believes that the sheer clout of her own authority or her purely judicial measures will discourage further inadequate parental behavior toward children.

This does not mean that each professional ought to disparage and abandon his own tools as being partial or consider them inadequate and devote himself to other skills. Such a mistake, frequent even in other operative contexts, would be irreparable in situations of violence, which, given the numerous aspects of the problem, require diverse approaches and interventions. We should not forget that in order to delineate the problem of family violence in a complex and dynamic way, we have to survey a constellation of critical factors and events—legal, medical, social, and psychological (Bertotti & Malacrea, 1987). Individual modes of operation prove indispensable by virtue of their specific natures, so long as they can all be integrated in a unified program that both encompasses and utilizes them (Masson, 1981, 1988).

For example, the way in which a family uses economic assistance not only offers useful information to the psychologist performing the diagnostic evaluation, but also becomes a different operative procedure for the social worker if he as acquainted with the dynamics underlying the couple's economic management. Similarly, the description of a home visit that reveals disorder and confusion is useful not only to the social worker; it can also show the psychologist that the wife, instead of giving up her vindictive desires toward her husband, finds an outlet for them by neglecting the household. Or take the worker who limits parental visits for the child's sake. Her measure is more effective if she offers both the minor and the parents a specific explanation, drawing on material obtained from the psychologist who is treating the couple for the difficulties they encounter during this particular phase of therapy. In this sense, the integration of the various approaches requires simultaneous efforts and a constant exchange of information. All these efforts have the same focus: to determine whether the relationship between the parents and the child can be restored.

The First Contact with the Family

The institutional framework has been clearly defined and the court has consulted the specialists; only now can the agency assigned to do the evaluation start the diagnostic process. At our Center, this process is laid out in a systemic and interactive perspective shared by all members of the team (see Chapter I, p. 7).

The Family File

The first step, whether in a private or in a public environment, is to set up a family file. This file contains a set of preliminary data useful for drawing a picture of the family's organizational patterns. Without such information, we run two different risks: we might be overwhelmed by the family's characteristic relational modalities without managing to verify them; or, vice versa, we might put the family through a boring initial session devoted entirely to gathering information.[4]

There is also the more serious danger that if we are in the dark prior to our first meeting with the family, we might find it impossible to organize and formulate preliminary conjectures that would be tested in the course of the session. Hypothesis, as we know, is one of the most effective tools for conducting a dialogue and certainly a basis for understanding a family's problems.[5]

If a psychologist is unable to formulate a hypothesis about an abusive family, she runs a further risk: She may be paralyzed by the family's reticence or confused by its denials. Thus, the knowledge of the salient elements characterizing the family's background and the elaboration of conjectures about the reasons for the crisis are even more indispensable in an abuse situation. Indeed, the hypotheses offer guidance in getting at the heart of the psychological problems that cause disturbance and suffering.

These factors necessitate the gathering of preliminary data, to be

---

4. In regard to the use and procedures of compiling a family file in a private context, see Di Blasio, Fischer, & Prata (1986, pp. 5–17). Useful information on the first contact with the framework of a public agency is to be found in Covini et al. (1984, pp. 62–68).

5. According to the definition supplied by Selvini Palazzoli et al. (1980), the systemic hypothesis "includes all members of the system and furnishes a supposition on the overall relational functioning" (p. 11).

summarized in a document with which the team prepares for its initial meeting with the family. Such information, which concerns the family unit itself as well as the parents' families of origin, is collected by the Center's social worker with the help of both parents during a home visit or, more rarely, by telephone.

The relational file is usually arranged in terms of several areas that clinical experience indicates as being the most significant. It is both inappropriate and useless for us to pile up an overabundance of detail on the pretext that we wish to know everything right away. On the average, at least according to our experience, a 20-minute dialogue would be enough to pinpoint the main relational elements.

In the normal practice of family therapy, aside from obtaining simple official data about the nuclear family and the parents' families, we explore certain causes of more or less latent conflicts: for instance, work, especially the wife's work; possible changes in or interruptions of either spouse's work; frequent job-related transfers or travels; transfers or relocations of the family; the sharing of space with or the close proximity of parents and/or other relatives. Close attention must be paid to these other persons in the household. They are, in effect, members of the family nucleus, part of the family system in every way and, as such, they can contribute to maintaining the family crisis expressed in every symptom, including, in this specific case, violence.

When investigating the extended family, we must try to determine whether any of the grandparents play a vicarious parental role with the grandchildren, or whether there are any interfamilial coalitions: either simple alliances (say, that of a grandfather with his own daughter) or cross alliances (say, that of a father-in-law with his daughter-in-law). A dysfunctional element of that type would allow us to hypothesize the existence of a sort of alternative nuclear family, in which the parental roles are assumed by a grandparent and one of the parents to the exclusion of the latter's spouse (Di Blasio, Fischer, & Prata, 1986).

In regard to the picture of the abusive family, which is often an irregular or multiproblematic family, we have added more details about several potential problem areas. Some of these may be: the presence of children from earlier marriages, their legal position in the current family unit, the ways in which separated parents relate to one another about raising their children, the recourse to institutionalizing children, any parental experiences of being abused or institutionalized during childhood.

The totality of information summed up in the family file constitutes a precise tool, allowing us to sketch an initial and temporary map of the family's interrelationships. We can then decide which members to invite to the first session, and we can formulate hypotheses, which are to be tested during our meeting with the family.

By now, the usefulness of formulating and verifying a hypothesis is an established fact. On the other hand, experience has demonstrated that "the most complex explains the most simple" – i.e., phenomena typical of the nuclear family are examined in the light of the complexity of the extended family (Ricci, 1981; Ricci & Selvini Palazzoli, 1984). This means that the diagnostic process must start by extending the analysis to more complex levels, so that an early session includes not only the nuclear family, but also the rest of the household as well as other people who may be involved in the problem. During later sessions, the evaluatory work can be limited to two persons or just an individual, so long as the more complex levels have already been explored.

Thus, the family file not only helps us to determine which level of the extended communication network (Ricci, 1981) to start on, but also allows us to formulate an initial hypothesis about the "pathological game." For the preliminary interview, in which the file is set up, we must follow the basic rule of maintaining a neutral position in order to discourage the family member from resorting to any possible manipulation or alliance.

In regard to drawing up the family file, the dialogue is necessary for a number of reasons: We have to review and reframe the terms of the problem as well as gradually widen the investigation to include the absent members of the system. To this end, we absolutely must avoid those areas that might prompt the interlocutor to comment on and evaluate the behavior, the opinions, and the feelings of absent members. The caseworker must therefore elicit a description purely of facts and conduct; in the course of the dialogue, he must request information actively and never just receive data passively. With skill and tact, he must be able to counter the client's linear logic by focusing on the web of relationships.

Who Should Be Invited to the First Session?

One of the goals of the family file, as we have said, is to help us determine whom we should invite to the first session. This summoning of family members constitutes an outright intervention, the therapeutic potential of which will be clarified in Chapter VI.

At a private center for family therapy, the range of people involved in the family's problem is usually limited to the network of relatives. We therefore have to summon them in order to probe specific hypotheses about the pathological game that supports the given symptom. On the other hand, a public agency cannot always initiate meetings with the certainty that the context is so clearly and precisely defined. In fact, we know that the context of a "public" intervention involves personnel in other agencies, who remain in contact with the family as individual therapists for a member of the family unit, as a support system, or to make referrals. In abuse cases, as we have amply explained in the preceding paragraphs, the *metacontext* of the evaluation is extremely relevant if not indispensable.

From this viewpoint, we must always bear in mind that in deciding on the makeup of the first session, we give priority to the contextual elements over those elements most closely linked to the family game. Thus, in situations in which several prerequisites for the "mandated assignment" are vague or lacking, we must devote part of the first diagnostic meeting to defining them. At the same time, we have to make sure that the session does not turn into a debate on abuse. The report on the abuse may be ambiguous: for instance, a medical profile that only hints at violence, a school report that aims more at forestalling parental hostility than at protecting the minor, etc. We then have to counterbalance this vagueness by using the information gathered by the social services in order to make the parents accept responsibility. In such cases, which are anything but rare, it is very useful to have the first session include the district social worker, who will actively collaborate with the center's psychologist not only in clarifying the context of the diagnosis, but also in underscoring the evidence that indicates episodes of abuse.

The presence of the social service or the custodial agency is likewise crucial if the scope of the abuse is not serious; the court may then assign the minors to the agency without requiring their removal from their parents. However, such assignment could make the family mistakenly assume that entering treatment constitutes sufficient grounds for a decrease or cessation of monitoring by the social agency. For this reason, the first diagnostic meeting must define the different, albeit integrated, tasks of evaluation and monitoring to be carried out by the two agencies.

In such instances, our first session aims primarily at defining the boundaries of the context, and then, only after this step, at partially testing our hypotheses about the psychological and relational roots of the violence. Hence, this primary meeting, important in and of itself, also serves as a preparation for the next meeting. The latter, which often includes the members of the parents' families, begins to gradually trace the background and reframe it; this meeting offers the family a reading that is different from the prevailing one. Frequently, we have to analyze the relations with the families of origin not in one, but in two separate meetings, each respectively with the maternal or paternal grandparents.

In an ideal situation, which can be realized by means of some exacting preliminary work, all the prerequisites we have discussed are not only implemented but already clarified to the family. At such times, we can accelerate the diagnostic process by having the first meeting include a member of the kinship network, a relative who seems to play a significant role in the abuse dynamics. It must be specified that this is usually possible in cases of neglect and physical violence, of which the network of relatives is amply informed. On the other hand, greater caution is advised for dealing with incest and sexual abuse: Secrecy and embarrassment often surround these situations even after a complaint has been filed and judiciary proceedings have begun.

It makes no sense to fight this reserve without the consent of the victim, who may not willingly accept the spread of information about herself—information that might put her in a bad light.

If parents are separated, we find it useful to meet individually with each once, since our primary goal is to determine which is the significant group in the dynamics of violence. Many such spouses, although living apart—often for years—nevertheless continue to maintain strong but confused and ambiguous ties by exploiting their children as instruments and/or extending the conflict not only to members of their own families of origin but even, at times, to professional who have made futile attempts to intervene. In such cases, the decision about whom to invite to the first meeting takes on the significance of an actual intervention. Among all the people involved, we have to choose those most directly implicated in the problem: for example, both parents and a member of the kinship network; or each parent separately and accompanied by the relative with whom he or she has the most intense bond. In any event, it is always better to spend time and energy on the preliminary gathering of information than to make gross blunders in the choice of whom to meet with during the first session—e.g., unimportant or peripheral relatives in the kinship network or, even worse, family members whose hostility is so great as to prevent any cooperation with the therapist.

Management of the First Session and Defining the Mandated Context

At the first meeting, after receiving all the family members who have been summoned and perhaps any professionals who are involved, we might find it useful to proceed as follows: Before tackling the more properly psychological aspects, we begin by clarifying the boundaries within which the evaluation takes place.

In fact, as we said initially, it is only within a clear context of taking charge—i.e., a sphere that actually utilizes rather than negates the coercive and prescriptive elements—that we can begin the psychological work of evaluating and perhaps treating the family in question.

During the first meeting, there are essentially four elements that are explained to the family members; these four elements define the boundaries of the mandated diagnosis.

1. The first boundary is drawn by the precise establishment of all the objective and concrete data attesting to the abuse that has occurred. To this end, we read the teachers' statements, the medical reports, the police records, etc. In the absence of objective proof, which is often lacking in our actual experience, it may be useful, as we have said in the preceding paragraph, to include the social worker who has referred the case or who is acquainted with it and has been following it. His testimony becomes a valuable factor, discouraging the family from denying or downplaying the events.

2. The second aspect defining the compulsory therapy consists of informing the family that the members of the therapeutic team have to act as advisors for the Juvenile Court, which is charged with issuing the final verdict on the fate of the minors. In our experience, reading the court decision aloud in the presence of the entire family clarifies the terms of our Center's responsibility. This prevents the family from viewing us as being willing to form an alliance against the court, which, in fact, is defined as our only and true referent. At the same time, we are sending a message of vital importance to the family: that, for the moment, our goal is neither therapeutic nor curative.

Categorizing the family members as "patients" would be tantamount to labeling the abusive parent as sick and thereby exempting her from her legal responsibility. Quite the opposite, full responsibility must be assigned to the family as a whole, and abuse must be defined as the expression of a crisis imprisoning all the members and causing distress and suffering. It is, once again, the psychologist's task to determine whether the family has the resources and the willingness to surmount this crisis. Finally, the family is informed that, at the conclusion of our work, a report will be forwarded to Juvenile Court. The family is given advance notice that prior to sending our report to the judge and to the supervising agency, we will invite the family to listen to our report, to ask for clarifications, and perhaps to comment on it. Anticipating that we will return a sort of assessment we thus achieve, among other things, the positive effect of reassuring the family members that no decision will be made behind their backs. Such a guarantee is even more indispensable within a structure like ours, which, although compulsory, is explicit and straightforward.

After various experiments, this practice struck us as the most satisfactory, because it allows us to take up a clear position between the referral agency and the client. The family is thus made to realize that we will punctually and unreservedly inform the judge of everything transpiring in our work together. Nevertheless, the family will still have a certain possibility of verifying our relationship with the court. We are virtually transparent on both sides: Our intervention with the client takes place in full view of the judge, and our relationship with the judge is visible to the client. This arrangement overrides the problem of professional secrecy—a notion that is completely inapplicable within a mandated context.

3. The third element is the declaration that the team, although about to commence its evaluation of the family, is going along with the court's temporary decision to remove the minors from the family unit (or entrust them provisionally to the responsible agency). The clarification of this point has the goal of confirming the importance of a court order that, while aiming chiefly at guaranteeing the safety and protection of the minor, also has the effect of inducing the family to deal with the true gravity of the situation.

The removal of children has a great strategic importance; mobilizing all the resources of the family, this step often overshadows the acute conflicts of the parents, who now cooperate in the joint objective of getting their children back. Usually, when we take charge of a case, we ask the court to remove also any non-abused siblings from the home, at least in high-risk situations. There are two reasons for doing so: We want to prevent any transfer of the abuse to another child and we want to avoid reinforcing the identification of the battered child as a scapegoat.

4. Finally, we have to clarify the relationships among the family, the specialized center, and the district agencies involved in the case. The proper tasks of the monitorial apparatus (the court usually names the social service) have to be defined; such tasks are distinguished from the evaluative and diagnostic duties of our Center. These measures lay the foundation for reinforcing the interinstitutional integration; every agency views the Juvenile Court as a higher authority to which it has to report. We explain this arrangement to the family members in order to prevent them from trying to manipulate or distort information or from dealing separately with the individual agencies. Throughout the diagnosis, we obviously have to demonstrate the significance of this collaboration. Our Center will do so at the diagnostic meetings by openly utilizing all the information about the family as the monitorial services gradually send us reports between sessions.

By clarifying these four aspects, we can tackle the problem of abuse from a position that is uninfected by a blurring of the context or by premature therapeutic expectations or intentions. Our Center's court-mandated task is to understand and explain the reasons for the crisis and to furnish prognoses about the risk of repeated violence. In line with these premises, we ask the family to supply concrete proof that no further abuse will occur. In complex cases that pose a high risk for a minor, we feel that only hard facts and real changes in behavior toward the children can be viewed as fairly reliable prognostic factors.

In technical, that is, procedural terms, the diagnostic sessions do not differ substantially from the therapeutic ones. Developing according to the criteria of hypothesis, they always follow a preparatory meeting, during which we reexamine the family file or the summary of the earlier meetings as well as the information obtained from the social service between meetings. These diagnostic sessions, which also include those members of the kinship network that are involved in the family, generally take place once a month; each time, we conclude with an intervention that focuses on the main issues raised during the session.

Relationship Between Coercion and Motivation

As we have said, we could not get to abusive families without legal coercion; yet it is likewise true that no one has ever been cured by a pure and simple coercive intervention. Thus, in their relationship with the clients, the therapists not only have to take monitorial steps to protect the child, but must also employ clinical instruments more suitable for grasping the pathological game and for getting the various members of the family unit to understand the tragic dynamics they are trapped in. The therapists therefore must, so to speak, "bewitch" the family; they must show that they are capable of understanding the family's complex functioning. By so doing, the therapists can give the patients sound reasons to hope that, by working together, they can find a way of escaping the vicious circle in which the family finds itself.

In their most recent work, which we have frequently quoted, Selvini Palazzoli et al. (1989) illustrated that in order to "bewitch" a family, the therapist has to play "anticipatory games." She cannot rely solely on the scant material that the family members grudgingly give her. On the contrary, she has to break through their barrier of reticence by asking highly precise and specific questions and even venturing to make intuitive statements when the appropriate information seems to be lacking.

It is obvious that such statements are based on the game hypothesis, which the team has constructed on the basis of preliminary data and experiences with other families having similar configurations of games. With our highly reticent abusive families, the "anticipatory game" is absolutely necessary. By checking the transcription of a session, we can see an example of these transactions between the therapist and the family.

The following is a very serious case of psychological abuse, in which the trauma endured by two children, seven and eight years of age, is the type known as "witnessed violence." The children were involved in several angry parental quarrels, which regularly culminated with the father beating the mother. The meeting excerpted here was the third.

This time, the children (who, several months earlier, had been sent to a shelter several miles from Milan) were not present, because, at the previous session, they had again witnessed a violent scene between their parents. Mrs. Bisceglie, who had shown up at this session alone, with a black eye and a swollen nose, had said that she had separated from Mr. Puglisi for the nth time. Her mate, who arrived several minutes late, liquored up, had coarsely hurled the house keys and a check at her, and, mouthing gross insults, he had declared that he never wanted to see her again. As a result, they were given separate appointments. She came with a sister, who had been helping her economically for years; he came with his stepmother, with whom he moved in whenever he left his companion. However, during the interval between the second and the third appointment, the two parents had notified the district social worker that they were again living together in their stormy fashion, alternating between the vociferous breaks and precarious reconciliations that had characterized the past four years of their long relationship. That was why our team had decided to summon them to a joint session, along with the woman's sister, Carmela. This time, Mr. Puglisi arrived first and alone. Grumbling, he explained that he had refused to drive the two women over in his car because he had gotten angry at "Bisceglie" (each partner always referred to the other by his or her last name). The two sisters, compelled to use public transportation, arrived 40 minutes late.

The therapist, making a superhuman effort, began the meeting by having them describe their latest fight. Mrs. Bisceglie sat motionless in her corner; verbally and nonverbally, she was as communicative as a mass of granite. In the other corner of the ring, Mr. Puglisi was far more interested in pursuing the fight than in answering the therapist's questions. In the middle was the sister, who tried to act nonchalant, giggling in embarrassment and minimizing what had happened. Finally, the therapist managed to elicit that Mr. Puglisi had lost his temper because Mrs. Bisceglie had responded to a man who had greeted her on the street, a stranger to her mate. She had then reacted poorly to Mr. Puglisi's remonstrances, Carmela had defended her, and "Puglisi" had kicked "Bisceglie" in the middle of the street, then driven off in his car, leaving the two women in the lurch. We will now transmit the subsequent dialogue between the therapist and the three people:

THERAPIST: (to Mrs. Bisceglie's sister): Carmela, how long ago did you realize that Mr. Puglisi is jealous of you?

CARMELA: You didn't understand me. He got mad at her because she greeted a man on the street.

THERAPIST: I got it, I got it, I'm not deaf. But don't imagine that I would believe such garbage! Mr. Puglisi can't possibly believe that his wife goes to bed with every man who says hello to her in the street! It's *you* he's jealous of, he's jealous of the relationship that your sister Assunta has always had with you. (Assunta laughs.)

CARMELA: My sister is always calling me, asking me for help, telling me, "I'm breaking up with him, I can't stand Puglisi any longer, he doesn't work, he drinks, and when he drinks he gets nasty," and then I tell her, "Break off with him" but she doesn't do it.

MR. PUGLISI: If I drink, I've got my reasons, and don't think she's got nothing to do with it!

THERAPIST: (to Assunta): But today, did your husband—excuse me—did Mr. Puglisi drink *after* that scene, before coming here, or had he already been drinking when you began to fight? (Assunta looks at Mr. Puglisi and does not answer)

MR. PUGLISI: (threatening): What do you mean "drinking"? Do I look like I've been drinking?

THERAPIST: Yes, you do, I'm not the least bit blind, and my nose is functioning!

ASSUNTA: (reassured by the therapist's words): He had already been drinking, he starts drinking in the morning. . . .

THERAPIST: (to the man): Were you drinking because you were angry that your wife—excuse me, I keep making that mistake—because Mrs. Bisceglie would be coming here with her sister?

Mr. Puglisi launches into a lengthy and confused discourse: It seems that when Mrs. Bisceglie acquired the home where she wanted to live alone, but where she is nevertheless putting him up, she preferred to borrow the money from her sister rather than from Mr. Puglisi, who would have gotten it from a customer (Mr. Puglisi is a house painter).

THERAPIST: (to Carmela): But you, Carmela, don't you realize that your sister is using all the help you are giving her in order to destroy herself? She's like a drug addict throwing away her life, and you keep giving her money for drugs. . . . Yes, your sister has no intention of getting better, settling down, finding happiness. . . . All she cares about is showing her mother in Puglia what a disgusting life she leads!

ASSUNTA: But I tell my mother nothing about these things! I only visit her in the summer to see my children! (Mrs. Bisceglie has two adolescent children by a previous man; her mother has legal custody of the children.)

THERAPIST: But Carmela keeps telephoning her and keeping her informed, isn't that so?

As we can see, the therapist has taken three great risks in this passage: "Carmela, how long ago did you realize that Mr. Puglisi is jealous of you?" "Did your husband drink before or after?" "Your sister is throwing her life away in order to make her mother see her do it!" Yet these are not unfounded maneuvers. Wild guesses are the only method for extracting information from people who are completely unwilling to furnish it freely. If the anticipatory game turns out to be wrong, the family members, disagreeing with the therapist, will be forced to come up with their own versions. In this way, spurred on by their anger, aggression, or emotional participation, they will communicate some shred of truth.

Bear in mind that only the second of the therapist's guesses ("Did he drink before or after?") is typical of the highly evaluative context of the mandated treatment. Here, in fact, the client tries to deny his own alcoholism to the therapist and, through the latter, to the judge, since his children have been removed because of his violence during drunken spells. But in regard to the therapist's two other attempts to expose the game ("He's jealous of her sister"; "She is only thinking about her mother"), the reticence of each family member is aimed not at the therapist but, primarily, at the other family members. Like a malign tumor, the pathogenic game develops silently, invading the family's relational nerve centers. As we shall see in the subsequent chapters, the goal of unmasking this game makes nonvoluntary treatment similar to spontaneous family therapy.

In either instance, beyond the falsehoods and manipulations expressly aimed at the therapist as the ally of the court, the various family members "lie" to one another. They all conceal their own intentions and strategies, because they have given up all hope of being understood and supported by the rest of the family.

This is the reason why the court-mandated therapist avoids the depression she would feel if she believed she were betraying her role of healer by turning into an inquisitor, who wrings careless admissions from a client in order to use them against him. Exposing the "cancer" is crucial to the process of extirpating it. If the therapist understands this, she can also make the patient grasp that his passive resistance to the coercion can be replaced by a genuine desire to cooperate in the treatment.

IV | THE DIAGNOSIS OF THE ABUSIVE FAMILY

What We Mean by Diagnosis

THE PSYCHOLOGICAL EVALUATION requested by Juvenile Court can be briefly defined as an advisory action to supply additional material for shedding light on a controversial and contradictory problem regarding minors. Obviously, the psychologist's advice is not requested if the facts are clear enough for the judge to reach a quick and immediate decision.

These basic conditions, which characterize most requests for expert opinions by psychologists,[1] are joined by a specific element characterizing cases of family abuse and violence: the fact that physical or mental violence inflicted upon minors may call for the application of penal laws, that is, lead to prison or fines for the perpetrator.

---

1. A lengthy and interesting treatment of the various types of expert opinions (psychiatric, psychological, on the responsibility of the juvenile, the alcoholic, the drug addict, on posing a danger to society, on the injured party, on a witness, etc.) was written by Gianluigi Ponti (1987) in four chapters of *Trattato di psicologia guidiziaria* edited by G. Gulotta. To clarify the difference between expert opinions in criminal proceedings and official technical consultation in civil proceedings, see Ponti, op. cit., "La perizia psichiatrica e psicologica nel quadro della legge penale" (pp. 593 ff).

The request for verification in cases of this type signifies that the Juvenile Court judge—using the penal procedure that an ordinary court can decide whether or not to initiate—has decided to invoke civil legislation, whose instruments are different from punishment. Such instruments, as emphasized by Ammanniti et al. (1981), allow for a timelier and more flexible intervention. Not only do they offer the possibility of forfeiture or suspension of custody, but they also have a potential for diagnostic, therapeutic, or welfare interventions.[2]

Thus, the request for verification constitutes an alternative—and/ or parallel—to the penal procedure. Its binding character, which is such that no family would dare ignore it, is established by temporary orders issued by Juvenile Court and accompanied by and including the limitations on parental custody (articles 330, 333, and 336 of the Italian Civil Code). In this sense, we may say that the removal of minors from their parents, along with orders for assessment of cases involving abuse of violence, represents a clear constraint by Juvenile Court in dealing with a family. Such constraint, although explicit, is, in substance, no different from the implicit constraint typical of expert opinions regarding child custody (for example, in cases of hostile separation of spouses). If one parent refused to go along with an evaluation arranged by the court, then he would be offering the court anything but a positive statement about his motives for taking care of the child. Hence, even other requests for a psychologist's opinion are characterized, although less patently, by the presence of strong elements of constraint.

2. Within the context of applying the civil code, the loss of custody in child abuse cases "presents notable differences vis-à-vis the loss of custody in Criminal Court, where it constitutes an additional punishment for certain crimes: rape, sexual offenses, corruption of minors, obscene acts, kidnapping, incest, and other offenses against the legal status of a child. The additional sanction is an automatic consequence of a sentence, while civil loss of custody can be declared by the judge. The criminal sanction applies to the custody of all the criminal's children, including those who are not victims of that crime; while the civil sanction purely concerns the relationship between the parents and the injured child. A criminal's loss of custody remains in force without amnesty or rehabilitation, while the civil loss of custody can be reversed if the causative circumstances are changed" (Ammanniti et al., 1981, p. 80).

The Psychologist Faced with the Family in a Mandated Context

The presence of explicit constraint obviously creates no small number of problems for the psychologist or psychiatrist, who is used to dealing with spontaneous requests and acting on the implicit assumption that the client is at least somewhat motivated and interested in undergoing and cooperating with diagnosis and therapy. Such an attitude is missing from a court-mandated situation. In this area, which, in certain aspects, is comparable to evaluation regarding child custody, professionals know that a couple's more or less explicit conflicts will prevent them from working toward a common goal. The tangle of confrontations, the exploitation attempts, the vindictiveness and mutual aggression get in the way, keeping the parents from focusing on a child's problems. Instead, they use their children as weapons in their competitive fight.

As Gulotta has emphasized (1983, pp. 2–3), the expert diagnostic opinion varies substantially from the clinical one. In the latter context, the client, aware that she is in trouble and wanting to be cured, makes a spontaneous appeal for help, while the therapist is committed to maintaining professional secrecy.

It must be noted, however, that situations involving these ideal conditions are less frequent than one might think. Requests for intervention in regard to a child or adolescent may come from parents or teachers; other requests may come from a spouse worried about her partner's mental health; likewise, reports may be made about psychiatric patients who are incapable of asking for help on their own. These are some of the instances often encountered by public service employees and by psychologists who must solve the problem of establishing the rules of the setting without, however, negating the validity of a request formulated in a nontypical manner. The evaluative situation concerning child custody is implicitly coercive, while the diagnostic situation in abuse cases is more clearly coercive; these two extremes are emblematic instances of problems shared by numerous appeals for psychological treatment.

On the other hand, the spread of psychological learning is accompanied by diverse and multifaceted demands that cannot be simplistically channeled into standard operating procedures, which are optimal and functional solely in the abstract or under particular conditions, such as in a private consulting room.

The Pretense of Spontaneity in a Mandated Context

Nevertheless, many professionals spend their energy trying to recreate the ideal conditions of private practice within a public context or in regard to "spurious" requests. Lacking a spontaneous request for help, they attempt to recreate those conditions in order to establish a rapport of trust and cooperation—convinced as they are that this is the only way to understand the actual problems of the clients.

Originally, we too proceeded along similar lines when making our first evaluative approach with an abusive family. But in the long run, as we shall see, we came to realize that this direction was ineffective and we abandoned it. Behind its barrier of silence and reticence, the family is entrenched in a complicity of massive denial of any abuse episode. These factors, together with our perception of internal torment and hidden conflict, represented very serious, indeed insuperable, difficulties. Feeling almost totally incapable of making any headway, the consultant was forced to work on a problem that the family refused to recognize as theirs. Hence, the need to gain the family's trust and spontaneity and to get the members to cooperate and discuss their relational problems and the roots of their crisis. This was possible, obviously, only if the consultant colluded with the family's denial and minimization of the episodes of maltreatment.

But this course soon proved to be a fiasco, because it had the absurd goal of pretending, come what may, that a mandated context was actually a spontaneous one. In most cases, the family was quite willing to discuss any topic so long as we respected the tacit agreement to avoid the painful subject of abuse. We thus came to realize that in a mandated context, we could not pretend to establish a rapport of trust and cooperation *as if* the therapy had been triggered by a spontaneous request for help. Furthermore, such make-believe inevitably led to our forming an alliance with the family against Juvenile Court, which implicitly appeared as a dictatorial authority that not only forced the family to knuckle under to an evaluation, but also compelled us to effectuate it. Aside from colluding with the family, a consultant may also run the opposite risk: She may take an inquisitorial and police-like stance, trying, at any cost, to get the family to admit and recognize that violence has occurred. If she does so, then, as we have noted, the family ultimately becomes our adversary, submitting to the court order and often, more or less covertly, distrusting us. As a result, the denials of maltreatment merely intensify; or else, if the parents do own up to the occurrence of maltreatment, they blame it on one another. Thus, the family eventually accentuates the dysfunctional patterns that sustain the root crisis of the violence.

Our anything but easy task is to sidestep the dilemma of collusion or inquisition, by trying to make the family see the possibility of a psychological solution that is free of manipulation, connivance, and legal judgment.

The definition of a context as mandated does not exclude the risk of a clinically inadequate approach; such a clear definition can, nevertheless, reduce this risk by helping the psychologist to avoid both an inquisitorial stance and a conniving attitude. It is obvious, as we will see in the subsequent chapters, that legal coercion is not a sure cure for the problems linked to violence. The point is that the family members can meet with experts, who, while in no way conspiring with them, understand and show that they accurately understand the dramatic ups and downs of the household—vicissitudes that, however, the family members (some more than others) sometimes consider so reprehensible that they feel they have to hush them up as thoroughly as possible. And it is only the knowledge of the family's specific ways of dealing with these problems, rather than an inquisitorial or judicial attitude, that distinguishes the position of the clinical psychologist from those of other professionals.

Why a "Photographic" Diagnosis Is Impossible

After avoiding the position of policeman and the pretense that the family has asked for help, we immediately face the next problem. How should we conduct and implement an evaluation, and which criteria and presuppositions should we choose? How can we understand the causes of the crisis and the maltreatment without tacitly supporting the family's denial and resistance? Also, what value and what meaning can we ascribe to statements made by people submitting to a court-mandated diagnosis? These questions require differentiated answers.

To start with, the social sciences have, by and large, jettisoned the idea that the psychologist, or for that matter any expert, can objectively evaluate and register the phenomena she observes and yet not be influenced by them and not emit, solicit, and be the privileged recipient of, certain messages.

Numerous studies have been done on the interaction that occurs between the examined and the examiner during clinical interviews and sessions. This research has demonstrated that whatever the examiner's role may be, he occupies an active position in a relationship of mutual influence. Yet in a seemingly more neutral situation like that of a patient undergoing psychological tests, we cannot assume that the results are determined purely by variables of personality and are independent of the overall situation. Such factors as the physical environment, the relationship between the examiner and the examined, etc., may influence the results that emerge and are observed (Bocchi & Ceruti, 1985; von Foerster, 1982).

In prescribed situations, hence in those requiring expert opinions or in mandated diagnoses of abuse cases, we must remember that the interview context is not the only one in which the interaction between the psychologist and the family takes place. The overall evaluation develops and crystallizes within a "metacontext" (Selvini Palazzoli, 1970) involving judges, consultants, agencies, and families—all of them with systems of often diverse ideas, knowledge, and expectations (Cigoli, 1983, p. 257).

Constraint per se does not invalidate the diagnostic outcome, provided we view the constraint as a framework for evaluating everything that emerges and comes to light.

Frequently, the expert observer tends to favor the aspects of content (e.g., facts, events, individual personalities, family relationships, etc.), driven as she is by the overriding and often illusory assumption that she can reasonably evaluate the ability of a family or of either or both parents to care for the children. In so doing, the evaluator underrates the scope of the "metacontext" in which the overall evaluative process takes place. An approach of this type, which claims that it can *objectively* judge the answers of individuals while disregarding the area in which they have meaning, could be valid only for opinions on inanimate objects—for instance, when gauging the level of food adulteration or the security of a house. But it will generally fall short of the goal of understanding relational problems.

Unlike inanimate objects, human beings are endowed with intentionality and cannot avoid strategic behavior, which is in some way connected to signals coming from the situations in which they find themselves. Thus, in a mandated context, people cannot avoid picking up on the psychologist's standards and expectations and displaying behavior—at least in their intentions—that is consistent with those criteria and suitable for achieving their own ends.

How, then, can the consultant make out the reality of what is presented to him; that is, how can he distinguish between that which is spontaneous and that which might be a response provoked by the given situation. As a result, the pretense of occupying a neutral position for registering and observing the answers collides with the impossibility of evaluating their significance. If you believe that you are in a position in which you can avoid influencing or being influenced, you lose your awareness of the effects of your own interventions. Hence, in our opinion, controlling our communicational behavior means having clear goals in mind while knowing that mutual manipulation cannot be avoided.

Today, the reflection on and subsequent deepening of these topics constitute inescapable tasks for the psychological sciences—if only because of the increasing demand for intervention in contexts and situations lacking a spontaneous and clear-cut plea for help. In regard to abuse cases, we must work out sufficiently plausible diagnostic and prognostic frameworks, in order to prevent any repetition of violence. This necessity has induced us to abandon any evaluation that is purely descriptive or based on the specialist's intuition. Our efforts aim at producing diagnostic and prognostic conclusions that are as lucid and verifiable as possible. Toward this end, we go essentially by hard facts and evidence attesting to a real change in the family situation.

Diagnosis as "Experimental Dialogue"

In our opinion (Di Blasio, 1988b), the diagnostic approach in a prescribed situation resembles the "experimental dialogue" that, as affirmed by Prigogine and Stengers (1979, p. 7), "involves both understanding and modifying the phenomena being investigated." Needless to say, experimentation does not connote cold, detached observation, nor does it mean abandoning the effort to empathically grasp the emotions, conflicts, and relational games in which the individuals are trapped. Furthermore, in using the accepted meaning of "experimentation" in the modern sciences, Prigogine and Stengers assert that "experimentation does not mean merely faithful observation of things as they happen, much less a simple investigation of connections between phenomena; rather, it presupposes a systematic interaction between theoretical concepts and observation" (p. 7). The experimental dialogue implies not passive observation but a practice in which the results acquire meaning only in reference to a hypothesis concerning the principles to which the processes are presumably referred (p. 41).

The application of these principles to the diagnostic situation might help us to escape the subjectivity of evaluation, which would then be referred to explicit intersubjective criteria shared by the family; these criteria would unite the level of understanding with that of change and modification.

According to these general principles, the diagnostician must not be content with observing and "photographically" registering the relational dynamics that characterize the family; she must also clearly and actively supply input that leads to change and movement. In other words, together with the rest of the team, she has to formulate one or more conjectures about the family game that supports and provokes the violence. If her hypothesis is empirically confirmed by the family's statements, we thus reach a first level of understanding: a necessary but not sufficient condition for triggering a change. In our eyes—and in the eyes of the family—only the connection between the level of theory and the level of concrete action can confirm the validity of any suppositions about the intricate and complex game in which the family unit is trapped; and only that connection can prove the family's ability or inability to interrupt the game.

In the case of a family that we shall call Neri, the mother was abusing her six-year-old son. One of our very first hypotheses, shared by the family itself, concerned the presence of a denied coalition between the husband and his mother—a coalition that, by completely excluding the wife, ultimately deprived her of any authority in raising the child. The boy, who was very close to his grandmother but disobedient and reactive toward his mother, would eventually provoke her impotent rage and sense of frustration, which were two of the causes of the maltreatment. However, the family's verbal confirmation of this hypothesis was not followed by any evidence that the pathogenic game could be terminated. On the contrary, the information we gathered, whether through sessions or through the efforts of the social service, indicated that the coalition between the boy's grandmother and his father was bound to persist. It was only after some two months that the wife had the courage to stand up to her mother-in-law and, simultaneously, the husband assured his mother that he respected his wife and considered her a capable and reliable mother. In this way, we saw our hypothesis substantiated by concrete behavior: It had been accepted and could generate a restructuring of the familial relations.

For a mandated situation, our diagnostic goal is to demonstrate by means of concrete facts the changes occurring in the family. The expert's role cannot be limited to that of a mere observer: He has to suggest different games to the family and various kinds of alternative behavior.

We should never forget that we are dealing with families that, given the situation, *must* reorganize their own interactive patterns. Not only do the family members have an overriding fear of losing their children, but they also wish to regain social credibility as a family and reacquire a private space without being monitored by the court or the social services. These factors are potent incentives for change—certainly no less potent than the motive for a spontaneous plea for help. However, if the family is left to its own devices, the dysfunctional patterns maintained in the typical game of abuse will change, but only superficially. We may thus add that the same external measures implemented by the services and the court to restrain or eliminate any risks of abuse are, potentially, utilized and incorporated in order to propose again, in a different guise, the same game typical of the crisis that unleashed the violence in the first place. Hence the risk that a pattern may become chronic; this is nothing but the consolidation of a dysfunctional game played by a growing number of participants inside and outside the family nucleus.

Thus, in our opinion, the psychological consultant who claims to be an observer "photographing" the family dynamics may unwittingly become a powerful ally of the dysfunctional game. If the diagnostician fails to assume an active role, then the family, which has no possibility of decamping, will adopt its only available choice: to manipulate in order to gain its own objectives.

A Case Exemplifying the Diagnostic Process

Let us now outline the case of a family, which we will call Ruggeri; the family was referred to our Center by Juvenile Court for diagnostic verification of the father's serious abuse of his three-year-old son.

In taking charge of the case, we created the context for starting the diagnostic meetings with the family in nonambiguous conditions. The two sons, the abused one and the firstborn, had been removed from the family and temporarily placed in an institution; the court order had been received both by the family and by our Center; the necessary information for preparing the first session had been gathered and summed up in the social and family file.

First Phase: Contextual Prerequisites and Formation of the Interinstitutional Team

At a plenary meeting of our team, we designated the operative micro-team to which the family was assigned. Since this was a case that did not directly involve the team's educators or instructor, we decided to delegate it to two psychotherapists and a social worker. The direct therapist would conduct the diagnostic talks, the supervising therapist would observe from behind the one-way mirror, and the social worker would maintain contact with the colleagues outside the Center who were part of the interinstitutional team: the Juvenile Court judge, the caseworkers at the agencies, the physicians, the residential workers at the institutions.

Before meeting with the family, the micro-team sifted through all the available information in order to sketch some initial hypotheses on the family's dynamics and to decide whom to invite to the first meeting. The following is our outline:

The Ruggeri family is made up of the father, Silvano, 28 years of age, the mother, Giovanna, 35 years of age, and two sons: Gianni, 13, from the mother's previous relationship, and Saro, 3, from her marriage to Silvano. Saro is the victim of the father's serious and repeated abuse during the mother's brief absence. The mother, upon noticing her son's injuries, was forced to have him hospitalized. On this occasion, the district social worker became aware of the case.

Silvano's family of origin is made up of a younger sister, Nina, 25 years of age, and their father, both of them employed. Silvano's mother died three years ago, several months after the birth of her grandson Saro. Silvano's parents, who had always been in conflict with one another, had separated about five years earlier. At the time of their separation, both children opted to live with their mother. Silvano sided with his mother to the extent of breaking off completely with his father.

Giovanna's family of origin lives in southern Italy, where she was born and where she lived until the age of 17, at which point she decided to look for work in Milan in order to escape her parents' constant fighting. Giovanna had her first child, Gianni, at the age of 22, by a man who died in an accident before the child's birth. Gianni spent the greater part of his first six years with his grandparents until Giovanna, against her family's wishes, decided to take him back permanently. Meanwhile, her younger brother, Guiseppe, now 33 years of age, had relocated to Milan, where he got married; together with his own family, he moved into an apartment next door to his sister's.

Three months after they first met, Silvano and Giovanna decided to get married, at Silvano's insistence, but against his parents' advice. Unable to find more adequate housing, they had no alternative but to settle in the tiny apartment where Giovanna was living with her son Gianni. The economic circumstances of Silvano's parents were anything but straitened; yet they never gave the young couple the least bit of assistance, either at the time of the wedding or later on.

After the wedding, Silvano tried to improve his economic situation by investing a small amount of capital in an enterprise that soon failed; now out of work, he was supported for four

months by his wife, who was already expecting a baby.
Silvano's unemployment was made more difficult by his mother's death, a traumatic event that sparked a deep depressive
crisis, inducing him to leave Giovanna and attempt suicide.
Subsequently, Silvano moved back in with his wife and found
a full-time job, which, however, was not up to his aspirations.

Pre-Session

The team analysis of this familial situation was the object of a long
discussion, during which we tried to hypothesize the reasons for the
crisis and for the mistreatment of little Saro. Among the various
conjectures, the one that struck us as most likely concerned the
relations between the Ruggeri family unit and Giovanna's family of
origin.

We wondered if Silvano's violent reaction might not be linked to
continual put-downs he received from his wife and to interference
from her family. Our assumption seemed to be corroborated by
several indications in the description of Giovanna's relationship to
her family of origin. For example, her parents' opposition to having
her son Gianni return to her could have been a sign of their low
opinion of her ability to take adequate care of the child. And, if this
conjecture was accurate, what role had her brother Guiseppe played?
Had he perhaps been given the job of protecting his sister from
possible mishaps and acting as the boy's father and protector? It was
quite possible that by moving to Milan and settling next door to his
sister, Giuseppe had taken over a number of monitorial tasks, which
he continued to perform even after Giovanna married Silvano. In
our talks with the family, we decided to start in with this topic and
then eventually to analyze Silvano's relationship with his family of
origin.

We decided to invite the social worker from the agency that had
reported the case to Juvenile Court to the initial session. We realized
that the hospital where the boy had been treated had drawn up an
extremely general medical diagnosis that offered no—or at best, an

implicit—hint of abuse. Such minimization occurs rather frequently. However, the district social worker had gathered data from the hospital, the doctor, and the teachers at the boy's nursery, and this information excluded any possibility of accidental injuries.

Second Phase: First and Second Meetings

At his first meeting with the family, the psychotherapist described the procedures for conducting the meetings, the use of a one-way mirror and a microphone, and the presence, behind the mirror, of a supervisory colleague and a social worker from our Center, to whom the case had been assigned. Then, by reading the court order, the therapist clarified the diagnostic task entrusted to him by Juvenile Court, the stages of the work, and the court-prescribed monitoring to be implemented periodically by the district social service. Next, the district social worker read her report on the abuse episodes, and the therapist impressed upon the family the need to understand the problems that had led them to a situation critical enough to provoke the father's outburst of rage and aggression against little Saro. When the social worker left, the psychologist resumed the discussion with the family; he realized that the requisite preliminary steps had in no way helped to defuse the atmosphere.

The discussion with the complete nuclear family took place in a climate of great tension. Silvano appeared highly anxious. His wife, tightly clinging to the two children, responded in monosyllables, strenuously trying to minimize the episodes of mistreatment.

Initially, Silvano tried to defend his right to privacy, then to depict himself and his family as victims of institutions and society, and finally, to justify himself by citing their difficult economic and housing circumstances; he consistently alternated between exhibiting aggressive arrogance and playing the victim. All that the therapist could glean from this torrent of useless words was that Silvano was deeply frustrated by his father's and his sister's disrespect toward him and by their unwillingness to help him out. This theme struck us as very important, but for the moment, the discussion bogged down in reticence and ambiguity. For one thing, because her husband monopolized the conversation, Giovanna was given very little space: He would answer questions directed at his wife, employing a more sophisticated and confused terminology to clarify anything that he felt his wife was incapable of explaining lucidly. He was obviously trying to relegate her to a subaltern position, one of inferior education. The therapist thereupon resolutely focused his attention on the wife in order to reconstruct her background, the events before and after her marriage.

In this way, he learned that Silvano had decided to get married against his parents' wishes in order to demonstrate to them that he was a real man capable of taking on the burden of not only a wife but also a child who was not his own. Hurrying to go through with the marriage and convinced that he would obtain the gratitude of Giovanna and her family, Silvano had not considered the, for him, unthinkable hostility of her parents and her brother. As a confirmation of the hypothesis advanced at the pre-session, it turned out that Giuseppe, Giovanna's brother, functioned as spokesman for their parents, who lived in the south, and as the protector of his sister's reputation, so that she had been forced to see her boyfriend on the sly. Neither the marriage nor the birth of their son had put even the slightest dent in Giuseppe's prestigious role within the Ruggeri family, to whom he had continually given aid, advice, and moral support in difficult moments and times of marital conflict.

For his part, Silvano had always been, and still was, very ambiguous toward his brother-in-law, who aroused in him feelings of anger, admiration, fear, and envy. He was incapable of opposing him openly or developing a peer relationship with him.

This information sufficed to make us realize the enormous

importance, in the abuse dynamics, of each spouse's complex relationship with Giuseppe. For the moment, rather than digging any further into this topic, we chose to save it for a later meeting that would include Guiseppe. Therefore, we asked the couple, especially Giovanna, to inform Giuseppe that we were requesting his cooperation and that he would, in any event, be receiving a formal invitation from our Center. The wife promptly guaranteed that her brother would cooperate, while Silvano looked perplexed, nervous, and dissatisfied with this decision, which he tried to oppose with a thousand excuses. In the end, he affirmed that recently, because of the Juvenile Court order and the removal of the children, his brother-in-law had been acting hostile during their encounters and missed no opportunity to openly accuse Silvano of being a bad father and an inadequate husband. Firmly insisting on the necessity of Giuseppe's presence, we concluded our first session without delving into the meaning of the criticism of the brother-in-law, because that would have inevitably jeopardized the climate of the next meeting.

On the date set for this second meeting, Silvano telephoned to communicate the impossibility of his brother-in-law's participation, but insisted that the session take place anyway. We suspected that it might be useful to reschedule the appointment to a day when Giuseppe could make it. And indeed, he proved fundamentally important in helping us to begin to understand the game played by the family. Observing Giovanna and her brother Giuseppe, we had the distinct impression of seeing a couple from which Silvano was excluded. The two siblings sat close together, giggled, and continued to talk and exchange glances of complicity. Giuseppe, utterly unfazed by his brother-in-law's presence, strengthened by his presumed alliance with his sister, and convinced that she could only be oriented toward leaving her husband, unequivocally offered to take custody of his two nephews. Silvano turned crimson with fury, let out some timid protests, and looked quizzically at his wife. But he seemed too intimidated by his brother-in-law and too unsure of what his wife was thinking to muster the courage to take a decisive position. Giovanna, on the other hand, froze into an attitude of mute surprise. It was thus revealed that Giuseppe was actually the bearer of a request from his own parents: they would be very happy to get back their beloved grandson Gianni, whose removal had left a gaping void in their lives.

However, no definite plans were made for little Saro's future. Giuseppe felt he could take him in, even though his wife had not clearly expressed her views on the matter.

A large portion of the meeting was devoted to analyzing this request from the grandparents; our goal was to elicit a clear position from Giovanna, who was provocatively told that she was dominated by her younger brother and her parents. This reframing had the desired effect. Giovanna at last found the courage to openly express her opposition to the separation and her desire to find a new basis for relating to her husband. Silvano, in turn, while still maintaining his ambiguity toward his brother-in-law, seemed reassured by the way his wife courageously took a position.

We concluded the session by affirming the need to work with the couple in order to determine their ability to stay together and take adequate care of their children. Giuseppe seemed disappointed and irritated by his "betrayal" by his sister, who had preferred her husband over her brother; however, Giuseppe had no choice but to accept the decision while continuing to exhibit a subtle disdain for Silvano as a man and as a father.

Third Phase: Final Diagnostic Talks

In the next three diagnostic sessions, we decided to focus on the evolution of the husband/wife relationship and on the couple's relationship with Giuseppe's family, but without forgetting the enormous importance of the personal and familial problems afflicting Silvano. The decision to highlight one aspect of the problem came from our evaluation: We wanted to begin eliminating those conflicts that seemed the most urgent, most pressing, and most directly connected to the abuse dynamics.

It was obvious to us that Silvano had played a far bigger part than his wife in constructing this complex family "game"—if only because he was personally responsible for the abusive behavior. Yet it was equally obvious that his preexisting personal problems had been joined by causative factors that had functioned as detonators. Our diagnostic choice was to gauge the scope of these causative factors and determine the possible solidity and accessibility of change. Later on, perhaps in a more properly therapeutic phase, we would analyze how the combination of Silvano's and Giovanna's personal problems had generated the difficulties besetting the couple and their relationship to their children.

We therefore concentrated our attention on events that were closer in time—essentially the ones involving the mutual decision to get married, Giuseppe's role, and the role of the families of origin.

During these sessions, the couple seemed more united. Silvano had resolutely abandoned his disparaging way of reformulating in more learned words everything that his wife said. Giovanna, for her part, no longer clung protectively to the children, and she often turned to her husband to consult him.

In short, we confirmed that Giuseppe's position in the Ruggeri family had always been more important than Silvano's. The latter, because of his youth, had initially sought advice from and acceptance by his brother-in-law, who struck him as a decisive, enterprising, and capable man. Giuseppe, who had always acted as a surrogate father to Gianni, assumed the same attitude toward Silvano, treating him like a son. From the very start, all of the Ruggeri family's major decisions, concerning not only the boy, but also their economic management, had been made jointly by Giovanna and Giuseppe, and Silvano had never dared to protest. Furthermore, Giuseppe had never shown much respect for his brother-in-law, not only because of Silvano's youth, but also because of his lack of economic enterprise and his difficulties in getting obedience from Gianni, who, in fact, treated him more like a contemporary than a father. Silvano had then tried to raise himself to Giuseppe's level, at least economically, by investing in an activity that, however, soon turned out to be unpromising. During that same period, the couple realized that a baby was on the way and, almost simultaneously, Silvano's mother was diagnosed as suffering from cancer, which quickly led to her death. For Silvano, the death of his mother, his only (presumed) ally in his family of origin, was an extremely harsh blow; he was so disturbed that he neglected both his wife and his job.

Thus began his quarrels with Giovanna, who, feeling ignored and unprotected by her husband, turned even more to her brother, calling upon him to defend her in her discussions with Silvano. Little Saro was born into this climate of family tension. Under the circumstances, Silvano tried to make up with his father and his sister; he requested their help, demanded his right to their economic support, and asked his sister to give him her large apartment, in which she lived alone. All he got were refusals. His father (who had always been hostile to Silvano for allying himself with his mother and playing an active part in her decision to leave her husband) not only offered him no help, but even refused to meet Giovanna and get to know his grandchild.

Silvano's sister, although willing to put him up at times of acute conflict with his wife, never gave him the help he asked for; instead, she urged him to be more active, thereby making him feel like a failure. In a clumsy attempt to solve his problems by resorting to the strategy of making his father and his sister feel sorry for him, Silvano forgot about his wife and little Saro. When he finally decided to get a permanent job, he was filled with rage, hostility, and vindictiveness toward his father and his sister, and he continued to present himself to them as dissatisfied and in need of help and economic support. Convinced that he had tried to help his own family and that he deserved respect for his new job, he turned to his wife and his brother-in-law, expecting their appreciation. Instead, as he was surprised to discover, not only did his sacrifices go unrecognized, but, in the meantime, the solidarity between the two siblings had intensified. Giovanna had lost faith in Silvano and kept consulting her brother about even the slightest problems. Giuseppe, for his part, spontaneously came running over from next door whenever he heard the couple arguing in loud voices: He would rebuke his brother-in-law and sometimes even raise his hand against him.

Silvano was now aware of his own position of weakness, his wife's lack of faith in him, and Gianni's disrespect toward him as a father. In dealing with his brother-in-law, Silvano began to nurture a hatred that was a blend of fear and powerlessness. He never dared to defy him openly, he never contested his reproaches, he even tried to obtain his approval. On the whole, he put up with Giuseppe in silence, pretending that it was Giovanna who was keeping her distance from him and ousting him from their home. It is obvious that these various tactics, which were used by Silvano and Giovanna in order to solve their problems, had the opposite effect of further aggravating their conflict.

And indeed, the serious episode of abuse inflicted on little Saro occurred during a phase of extreme tension in these dynamics. Once, in the presence of a large group of Giuseppe's friends, Silvano had seen his brother-in-law put his hand on his sister's shoulder and brazenly say about little Saro: "Look how beautiful our little boy is." Silvano had lacked the courage to stand up to his brother-in-law or his wife, who, moreover, seemed delighted by her brother's opinions. The fight triggered by that incident had compelled the wife to seek refuge, as usual, in her brother's apartment, while little Saro, awakened by the shouting, had burst into tears. Unable to control his anger, Silvano had ferociously beaten the child, leaving him black and blue.

The Diagnostic Outcome

By the end of this session, we had verified several changes foreshadowing a different relationship between husband and wife. Obviously, the session did not miraculously lead to Giuseppe's exit. After an initial stage of focusing on the problem, the couple needed some time to gauge the harmful effect of Giuseppe's constant interference; they had to perceive how difficult it was for Giovanna to keep her brother at a distance and, above all, to validate Silvano in the children's eyes. As for Silvano, it took him a long time to reach the point of being able to confront his brother-in-law unambiguously, presenting himself as a husband and father and acting like one.

The spouses were willing to understand and, most important, to adopt a behavior that defined and protected their own family; their conduct was reason enough for us to finish our evaluation with a positive prognosis.

The conclusion of the diagnosis coincided with an initial overall summing-up in tandem with the network of monitorial services, which confirmed a marked improvement in the couple's relationship and a greater serenity when they visited their children at the institution. The convergence of these observations led to the diagnostic report, which, besides describing what we viewed as the makeup of the abuse dynamics, underscored all the ongoing problems that required treatment. The diagnosis and the proposal for a therapeutic program were then submitted to the Juvenile Court judge. Our program called for a partial return of the children to the family, but with continued suspension of paternal custody, the assignment of the minors to the Social Services Department, and monitoring by the social service.

When the Prognosis Is Positive

An evaluative approach that, like the one presented above, tries to get beyond a mere description of phenomena is responding to two demands: It has to shed light on the causes of the violence and it has to furnish prognostic indicators regarding the family's likelihood of recovery. These indicators, as we have said, originate in the movements and changes that the family produces in its own internal structure.

These first changes per se obviously do not lead to overcoming such problematical obstacles. Nevertheless, they enable us to begin therapeutic work that, during the subsequent development, will go back over the previously broached themes. In this way, we can dissect them more thoroughly, grasping them in all their facets and in their less evident implications. Needless to say, each family situation is unique, not only in its characteristics, but also in the time it requires to bring about changes. In the diagnostic evaluation and the prognostic forecast, we have to take this uniqueness into account when designing a program that is suitable to the child's needs.

On the level of institutional intervention, a positive prognosis anticipates a series of measures that alter the family's position in regard to the social services and Juvenile Court. In concrete terms, this means that the judge is sent a first report that, in pinpointing the roots of the crisis and the evolution of the familial relations, highlights those elements of change that support the prognosis. On this basis, the report specifically proposes a program tailored to the situation of the family in question. In many cases of positive prognosis, the central point of the program calls for either a gradual rapprochement between parents and children or the return of the children to the family. Indeed, the very concept of positive prognosis implies that the family is regaining its ability to take adequate care of its children. In short, this means that the spouses are forming a certain parental alliance and a relationship of mutual trust—indispensable conditions for dealing satisfactorily with the children's problems.

However, the time span for restoring children to their parents varies according to the projected length of treatment. If dangerous conditions are present and a long recovery—some two or three years—is expected, a prolonged separation of the child is advisable. This raises the problem of sheltering her in such a way that she is not only protected but also assured of a healthy psychophysical development. A remedy that is not always easy, but that, if carried out properly, offers optimal results is to grant temporary custody of the child to a foster family. With a positive prognosis, the minor's family can accept this provisional solution because it does not find it threatening, and the foster family, from the very start, nurtures no hopes of eventual adoption (Cirillo, 1988). Indeed, on the basis of healthy competition, the child's family may be inspired to work more rapidly toward getting the child back.

Nevertheless, if the familial conflicts and/or difficulties are resolved by the couple's decision to separate, we can speak of a positive prognosis, so long as their decision is reached in a manner that is not excessively traumatic for the children. When parents are trapped in an endless game of bitter opposition that prevents them from either staying together or separating, the basic conflict can be resolved by a decision to terminate the marriage; this separation can be consensual or, more frequently, implemented at the initiative of one of the partners. In such a case, the therapeutic work aims at determining the ability of the one parent to care for the children and of both parents to cooperate in preserving a good image of the noncustodial parent in the eyes of the children.

What to Do if the Prognosis Is Negative

The diagnosis of the dynamics leading to the mistreatment can, nevertheless, result in a negative prognosis, with the family being seen as incapable of caring for the children. There are, essentially, two types of these situations. In one type, we realize immediately during the diagnostic phase that no positive sign of change is apparent in the family; in the second type, the initial positive diagnosis, and hence the prognosis, are subsequently belied by certain facts that emerge in the course of therapy, such as episodes of violence or obvious parental unfitness.

In cases of the first type, there may be numerous reasons for the absence of any sign of change. The negative prognosis may correspond to the family's desire to expel the child—an attitude that the family itself cannot or dare not express openly. In such instances, we have to work with the family unit in the presence of the child (her age permitting), so that the parents can honestly state their implicit rejection, thereby dispelling all ambiguity. Elaborating on the underlying causes of the rejection can trigger overly intense guilt feelings, regret, or other negative effects. In these situations, it is important for parents and children to be able to separate, temporarily or definitively, while maintaining, as far as possible, mutual images that are not excessively deteriorated.

Then there are the situations in which the negative prognosis—or better, a prognosis of non-treatability—is due to errors made in the phase of setting up the context for taking charge of the case.

An example of such a case was the one in which a report to Juvenile Court attested that a mother was incapable of caring for her six children, ranging in age from eight to sixteen. However, the court order calling for the removal of the minors was implemented solely for the four youngest; the two oldest, drug addicts who were sliding toward criminal careers, had repeatedly escaped from an institution that was unable to enforce restraint measures. As a result, the two oldest children were left at home, and they refused to move out—in the face of the indifference of the social agency and the powerlessness of the court.

In this situation, it was impossible to help the mother regain a normative authority role with these children, who could not be controlled even by the institutions. In other words, it was easy for the mother to complain about her difficulties with her oldest children, depict herself as a victim of their bullying, verbally demonize them, shrug off responsibility, and hide her own complicity with them behind the powerlessness of the agencies, which she had repeatedly asked to remove only the two oldest children from her home.

Last but not least, we must bear in mind that even the errors and limits of a diagnosis or its inconsistency with that type of family can interfere with a positive change. If we realize this in time, we can work out modalities of specific supervision or devise strategies allowing a colleague to take up contact with the family in question.

Cases of the second type, in which the repetition of violence is verified in the course of therapeutic treatment, are obviously more painful and more difficult to deal with—both for the family members and for the professionals working with them.

Emblematic of this connection is the case of two young drug-addicted parents who were seriously neglecting their one-year-old. Juvenile Court ordered the child, who was afflicted with a serious illness, to be placed in a small children's home. In the course of the diagnosis, the desire to get back their son had induced the parents not only to give up drugs, but also to become independent of their families of origin, both economically and in their living arrangement. All things considered, their constant visits to their son, which were pedagogically adequate, seemed to indicate a positive outcome. These changes, which remained stable for about eight months, persuaded the therapy team to organize a program giving the parents greater responsibility in the care of their boy. Juvenile Court, giving all due consideration to the development of the situation, issued an order that, aside from prescribing a therapeutic treatment, allowed the couple to keep the child on weekends and for several afternoons during the week. With the resumption of their parental responsibilities, the couple began to act reticent and tight-lipped during therapy sessions, to ignore the dispositions and schedules of the institution housing the child, and to disengage themselves from the child, who promptly manifested a number of symptoms, including anxiety, insomnia, and loss of appetite.

In a dramatic session in which these factors were examined, the couple admitted that they had gone back to drugs despite their attachment to their son. At this point, notwithstanding the couple's pressure and requests, we had to make them grasp the importance of prioritizing the welfare of their child, who required constant and continuous treatment in a stable and serene environment, which could be offered only by an adoptive family.

If a prognosis is negative, and the minor needs to be removed permanently from his family, then we have to find an alternative solution. In general, our efforts aim at preventing a negative prognosis from being tantamount to our passing the buck to someone else. This means that, whenever possible, we try to get the parents to understand their own difficulties and also to give priority to the child's right to be treated and supervised in an environment outside his family. If we find a married couple willing to take care of the minor, the court will often ask our Center to evaluate whether this concrete possibility can effectively solve the problems. As we can imagine, the family feels less threatened if the proposed alternative is custody with relatives or in an institution that allows the parents to maintain some kind of relationship, however limited, with their children.

On the other hand, it is impossible to reconcile support of the parents with protection of minors in cases requiring adoption as a solution. This often indispensable measure can terminate our relationship with the family, which views us as sharing responsibility for so drastic a decision. In any event, this decision is never made behind the backs of the parents; no matter how unfit, they are entitled to have their dignity safeguarded and to be acquainted with all decisions concerning them.

V | GAMES TYPICAL OF ABUSIVE FAMILIES

Peculiarities of Games That Involve Abuse

AT THIS POINT, by drawing on our clinical work of the past few years, we can delineate a typology of families with abuse problems. Obviously, this classification is not exhaustive. Nevertheless, we feel that by grouping our clinical observations into categories of family games, we can stimulate other professionals to formulate explanatory hypotheses about the specific games operating in the abusive families that they see.

Family therapists acquainted with the reconstructions of games in psychotic families, as depicted by Selvini Palazzoli et al. (1989), can observe that the games of abusive families that we are going to describe have many similarities with the above games. Naturally, this depends on the individual observer, in the sense that we ourselves have outlined the games of abusive families on the basis of the ones described in psychotic families and we have, therefore, partially followed those models. On the other hand, we believe that these two types of games share numerous features—a resemblance that cannot be due solely to the observer's viewpoint. Several crucial phenomena are similar: e.g., the presence of unresolved ties with the extended families or the involvement of children in a parental conflict.

We would therefore like to delve into the differences between the two sets of games that we are investigating: those that cause a psychiatric symptom in a child and those that trigger abusive behavior. In fact, we are not yet clear about the combination of factors that results in the choice of physical violence—as opposed to the rest of the vast repertory of available behaviors—by the families being examined.

Unquestionably, however, one of these factors is the context of learning. As we pointed out in the Introduction, the literature stresses the so-called "repetitive cycle of abuse": Adults who were childhood victims of mistreatment are more likely to display violent behavior toward their own children (Cirillo & Di Blasio, 1988). Aside from this individual factor, there are other elements that we could certainly pinpoint in an intrapsychic perspective: immature personality, impulsiveness, criminal attitudes, etc. Beyond that, the explanation for the emergence of abuse often involves sociocultural aspects, particularly the high level of stress caused by social marginality, unemployment, overcrowded and inadequate housing conditions, poverty, and a lack of education that limits articulateness in regard to solving conflicts.

On a familial level, the presence of one or both factors (individual and social) joins with a third component: the peculiar and obvious presence of the game of the abusive family. Unlike the covert and evasive game of the psychotic family, this dramatic and blatant game instantly catches the expert's eye.

In the psychotic family, the marital conflict is seldom open; and even when open, it employs "smokescreen" tactics. The two spouses never explicitly communicate about the fundamental causes of their marital problems. And this failure, to summarize briefly, constitutes the notion of "stalemate," which Selvini Palazzoli et al. have pinpointed as the root of every psychotic game.

On the other hand, the marital conflict in the abusive family explodes obviously and violently, often directly affecting the weak spots of each of the two adversaries.

Furthermore, in the psychotic game, the intricate network of alliances and coalitions is almost entirely concealed and denied. Seduction and instigation among the parents and the children are maneuvers implemented chiefly through subtle analogous messages of which the protagonists seem, at least partly, unaware. In contrast, the factions in an abusive family are, by and large, sharply defined and exhibited provocatively, indeed downright brazenly, so that a parent's violence is unleashed against the child who operates in the enemy camp. Emblematic is the case of incestuous dynamics: in the abusive family, they are acted out in more or less complete forms, protected by the silence of the two participants and, at times, by the complicity of the other family members. On the other hand, in some families with psychotic transactions, the same dynamics are limited to an intimacy that is only hinted at, as in cases of anorexia nervosa.

With these premises, we can begin to sketch the typology of abusive families. In so doing, we have to distinguish between two kinds: the family in which the role of the abused child can, for simplicity's sake, be considered negligible; and the family in which the children actively endeavor to maintain the game linked with the mistreatment.

The first category includes those families in which the abusive or, more often, neglectful parent presents herself as generally incapable of raising and looking after her offspring—usually one or more very small children. This set of games can be labeled as "parental unfitness."

The second category, in contrast, includes families in which the object of mistreatment—more frequent than neglect—is a specific child (rarely two children), while the other children are spared. In this group of families, the abused children are usually at least two years old and, as we shall see, their behavior reinforces the mechanisms linked to the infliction of violence. As we can easily guess, the family games that are detectable in these households are of the scapegoat type.

Parental Unfitness as the Message

By analyzing the first category of games, we can view mistreatment as signifying a call for attention aimed at the other spouse, who acts uninterested in the abusive parent.[1]

---

1. The move of attracting a parent's attention through one's own parental unfitness—a widespread ploy in families with problems—was amply discussed in a preceding work (Cirillo, 1986b).

Child-Beating as an Expression of Anger at the Spouse

We can recognize the addressee of this message chiefly in the other parent. We already explained this possibility in Chapter II: In discussing several abusive parents who spontaneously turned to our Center for help, we commented that such a failure to perform one's job as a parent could be read as a reproach aimed at the spouse. In these cases, the abusive parent can, obviously, be either the father or the mother, and the spouses may be living together or apart.

Nevertheless, in order to facilitate understanding of the game that we would like to illustrate, it would be useful to take an extreme situation in a manner consistent with our sociocultural context and to hypothesize as follows. The abusive parent is a single mother; the father walked out on the family some time ago. The mother's recriminations focus chiefly on the man's neglect of his paternal duties toward the child, but he turns a deaf ear to the desperate protests of the abandoned woman, who did not want him to leave in the first place. In a similar case, this latter aspect is concealed by the woman, who, if only out of pride, keeps obstinately reiterating that the *only* thing for which she won't forgive the traitor is his failure to live up to his obligations as a father.

The abuse of the child thus expresses an intricate tangle of feelings in which the mother is floundering. On the one hand, she hates the child, whom the treacherous father has dumped in her lap as a cumbersome burden so that he can enjoy life. While she probably wanted the child and loved him intensely so long as he was the fruit of a happy relationship, she now feels unbearably oppressed by him. On the other hand, she sometimes displays a stubborn urge—"I'll show him" (meaning her ex-companion): She takes care of the child with obsessive perfection, so that the father can see with his own eyes how useless he is and how little he is missed. But no sooner does the mother begin to feel inadequate for the enormous task of properly raising the child on her own than the boy is instantly transformed into the handicap that his father inflicted on her by walking out on them. If the mother then mistreats the boy, and seriously at that, she is aiming her aggression at him because she blames him for not responding affectionately to her attentions. The boy is thus the cause of her failed life; he is the chain that shackles her, the (unwitting) instrument of the traitor who left, but who, through the child, keeps indirectly persecuting her.

In less exacerbated circumstances, parental abuse of a child may be a reaction to emotional rather than physical abandonment by the spouse, who staves off requests for affection, closeness, companionship. Indeed, the traitor can neglect the spouse by burying himself in his work. In the two cases that we outlined in Chapter II (pp. 20–26), the wife's or the husband's escape into work was experienced as particularly unjust because it forced the spouse to assume the full burden of responsibility for rehabilitating a disabled child; the spouse did a conscientious job of caring for the child, but occasionally he or she would beat the child violently.

The traitor need not be a workaholic; he can betray his spouse with a rival, as in the following case.

In the family that was sent to us for an evaluation, the young father had savagely beaten his 18-month-old daughter, although he was patient and tender in raising his firstborn, who was now six years of age. Our reconstruction showed that when the young man had gotten engaged, his future father-in-law had warned him that his fiancée would be incapable of performing her maternal duties. She would require constant help and guidance, he said. The girl, who had always been considered slightly retarded, had grown up under her father's protective wing. The husband, first with their marriage and then with the birth of their first and second children, had harbored the illusion that he would replace his father-in-law. Instead, he discovered that his wife kept running to her father, asking for his guidance and advice, leaving her husband at home alone with the children, after work.

One day, the wife surreptitiously took money from her husband's pay envelope and brought it to the father/rival. This final provocation triggered her husband's furious outburst against their little girl, who embodied his acute failure to get his wife away from her father and definitively tie her to himself—efforts that he had pursued chiefly through the children.

When the Call for Attention Is Aimed at the Parent's Mother

Often, however, this communication—that is, the message saying "I am incapable of raising my children"—is addressed not to the spouse, but to a parent of the inadequate parent. In this situation, the abuse is frequently chronic but inconspicuous, rather than being acute as in the preceding cases, and it can manifest itself as serious neglect or carelessness.

An example will illustrate the most typical form of this situation. As we shall see, this is one of the few spontaneous cases that we have encountered. In line with what we have previously affirmed, this self-incrimination can likewise be seen as a kind of accusation aimed at another person.

Mariella, who came to our Center for help, lives with her two children: Sara, 20 months old, and Omar, six months old. Her companion, a North African, is in prison for pushing drugs. Mariella lives with her old paternal grandmother, who looks after Omar while Mariella works as an accountant in a rather precarious job. The little girl goes to a day-care center. Mariella has problems with Sara, towards whom she acts impatiently. The mother often beats the girl violently when Sara disobeys or gets dirty. Mariella, frightened by her own actions, would like to understand why she mistreats her daughter, whom she deeply loves; she would like to get help in order to change. A short investigation reveals that Mariella is the black sheep of her family, in which her two younger brothers have properly settled down. Her parents, still young, have been running a bar since her infancy, which is why Mariella was looked after by her paternal grandmother, who lived with them.

At this point, we set up a large session involving not only Mariella and her children, but also her parents and her grandmother. Our meeting readily brought out the animosity that Mariella had been harboring since childhood toward her mother, who spent little time with her. This hostility was exacerbated by criticism of her mother by her grandmother, to whom she was very close: Her grandmother put down her daughter-in-law (Mariella's mother) for preferring the hustle and bustle at the bar to her home and children. At the age of 16, Mariella began running away from home, and then did so more and more often. Next she turned to drugs, although she never became a true addict; she had various failed emotional relationships and briefly turned to prostitution. Mariella found a certain stability only with the father of her children; when he was incarcerated, she went to live with her grandmother, who had moved out of her son's home several years earlier because of conflicts with her daughter-in-law.

Through all these vicissitudes, Mariella never failed to keep her parents informed, usually indirectly, by confiding in the brother who was closer to her in age. Her parents were worried about her, but in her eyes they were only pretending: After all, the first time she had run away from home, they had waited a whole week before notifying the police.

In the above example, we can read Mariella's mistreatment of her daughter as one of many signals that she is sending to her own mother. It is as if the young woman were trying to implicate her, reprimand her, and punish her for having neglected Mariella as a child; and Mariella's own confession of abuse seems rooted in her desire to amplify that signal.

In general, when a mother exhibits parental unfitness in the hope that her children will be taken care of by *her* own mother, she is counting on obtaining a kind of indemnity for her own mother's neglect of her in her childhood. However, this maneuver is self-defeating. Should the grandmother refuse to look after her little grandchild, then the mother will be even more frustrated; and, since the child has failed to procure her mother's affection, she will take her rancor out on the child. If, on the other hand, the grandmother agrees to look after the grandchild, the mother will realize very soon that this compensation through an intermediary does not truly satisfy her: This is because the relationship between grandmother and grandchild tends to exclude her, leaving her feeling even more cheated of the love she wants from each of them.

Unfortunately, this situation is very common—for instance, in regard to children born to drug-addicted teenagers. The grandmother has been asked by her daughter, and perhaps appointed by Juvenile Court, to take care of the young mother's child. But then, almost without exception, the young woman has a breakdown as soon as the grandmother shows her love for the grandchild—a love that her daughter does not remember having ever received from her mother. Having failed with her own daughter, the grandmother virtually feels she has been given a second chance by her grandchild to realize her capacity as a mother. In order to devote herself completely to her new baby, she both physically and emotionally alienates her daughter, the embodiment of her failure.

We have consistently referred to female protagonists, because our experience has shown us that parental unfitness is a move typically employed by a young mother to call for her own mother's attention. This usually occurs in family configurations in which the young woman's father is absent or peripheral, or provides little support for either his daughter or his wife.

More often, the greatest display of neglect for which the daughter rebukes her mother is that she consented to her daughter's marriage. The daughter felt she had been "given away" to the first man to come down the pike, even though she herself insisted on marrying him. We can thus reconstruct the situation as follows. The young woman declared her intention of making an obviously bad choice of husband—this was one of numerous manifestations of protest, perhaps the most extreme, in her battle with her mother. In so doing, the daughter hoped that her mother would be completely averse to letting her go; by interfering with the marriage, the mother would have proved the validity of the bond that the girl had previously doubted.

Instead, after expressing not much more than perfunctory disapproval, the mother went along with her daughter's choice, thereby proving that she couldn't wait for the very first opportunity to get rid of the bothersome and exasperating girl. Given the choice of partner, the marriage collapsed. After such a failure, with all its foreseeable disappointments, the young woman may exhibit her inability to look after her children. So the grandmother agrees to take her in, at least for the sake of her grandchildren. At this point, however, the grandmother, despite having always criticized her daughter's husband, now advises her not to leave him, and refuses to assist her daughter. Her refusal forces the young woman to turn to the social services and request that they provide for her children. If the caseworkers comply without reading beyond the mere plea for help, they become unwitting surrogates for the grandmother. In that case, even though they may believe they are supplying only temporary assistance, they are actually promoting the conditions for chronic intervention: foster care, institutionalization, domestic support, etc.

Favoring One Child While Neglecting the Others

A third (and unusual) recipient of parental unfitness can be a child, typically the first, who has impudently become part of the married couple, while the other children appear, so to speak, outside the game.

A particularly striking example was a family that we will call Scalici. The couple eloped and got married at 15 years of age (a typical situation in certain areas in southern Italy). The youngsters then promptly had their first child, Vincenzo. The second child, Anna, died a few days after birth, so that the third child, Rosaria, was four years younger than Vincenzo. Two years later, Giuseppe was born, and then, the following year, Antonio. At this point, the family's relocation to Milan shattered the traditional couple pattern of their native culture, in which the father is the breadwinner while the mother raises the offspring and takes care of the household. Both partners found jobs, but with different schedules: he as a manual laborer, she as a cleaning lady; they divided the housework between them.

This latter point sparked their first conflicts, since the husband was reluctant to do "women's work" and was jealous of his wife's time outside the home. The wife, now 25 years of age, kept relying more and more on nine-year-old Vincenzo, to whom she would unburden herself about her husband's nasty character. Feeling more and more excluded, her husband turned to alcohol, thereby reinforcing the bond between mother and firstborn. Frustrated and incapable of clearly verbalizing his jealousy of his own son, the father simply impregnated his wife two more times. His wife reacted very badly to these two unwanted pregnancies. She tried, but failed, to abort the second one, though still continuing to work on the outside, while her husband kept drinking more and more and working less and less. He and Rosaria took primary responsibility for the four youngest children, thereby forming a couple opposite the mother/Vincenzo couple. However, while the latter bond was held together by an intense attraction, the father-daughter bond was cemented by rancor, jealousy, and envy toward the other two.

The symbolic marriage between the mother and Vincenzo was sanctioned by information that she received from their doctor that she communicated only to Vincenzo: The (titular!) head of the family was stricken with an advanced cirrhosis and had only a short time to live.

Meanwhile, Giuseppe, Antonio, and the two youngest children were growing up without adequate care from their parents. The mother was too bitter toward her alcoholic and violent husband, who did not work and whose only thought was to get her pregnant. Having lost his job, he was mortified by his overall domestic situation and, while drinking, kept complaining about the wrongs done to him by his wife. Vincenzo and especially Rosaria tried to get along as best they could, but the precarious equilibrium of the situation was suddenly disrupted when Vincenzo, now 16, found a girlfriend, Anna. His mother, terrified by the thought of losing her son's emotional support, tried to incorporate the girl into the family; she welcomed her with open arms as a reincarnation of her own dead daughter, whose name the girl coincidentally bore.

Anna, who likewise came from a ravaged family, was happy with this reception and did her best to deserve it by replacing Rosaria as caretaker of the youngest children. The father, for his part, was anything but unhappy to have someone relieve him of several domestic chores. The only dissatisfied person was Rosaria, who was ousted from her—shaky—identity as vice-mother to the family (and vicarious wife to her father). Needless to say, Anna soon tired of being a servant in someone else's home and began criticizing her future mother-in-law to Vincenzo, pressuring the boy to choose between them.

The social service workers, who had been assisting the family in regard to their most serious problems (poor performance at school, lack of medical care, vaccinations, etc.), now saw the condition of the family unit become more and more serious. Rosaria, who was repeating the second year of middle school but getting nothing out of it, would come to school in a more and more obviously depressed and confused state of mind. Giuseppe and Antonio, disoriented and disorderly, played hooky more and more often. The youngest children, who were attending kindergarten, were dirty, undernourished, and unhealthy. However, in their investigations, the social services ran up against the wall of parental denials, until Vincenzo made up his mind: accompanied by Anna, he went to the caseworkers and denounced his parents' neglect of his siblings.

In this family, the neglect can clearly be understood as a

symptom within a game that does not go beyond the confines of the family unit. The four grandparents were dead, and the various uncles and aunts, all of whom remained in the south, had little influence. The therapists who subsequently treated the family had the vivid impression that a game was being played by four players—father, mother, Vincenzo, and Rosaria—and that this game was then disrupted by the arrival of Anna. It seemed as if Giuseppe, Antonio, and the other two children (whose names, not coincidentally, were not mentioned) did not even reach the existential condition of players, either in their own eyes or in the eyes of the other family members.

When the social services took charge of the family, they removed all the children, excluding Vincenzo, who was now of age. At the first diagnostic sessions, which exposed the game that we have described, we had to contend with a totally unexpected reaction from Rosaria. She fled the institution where she had been placed, and she then had a dissociative crisis at the next institution. As we had already worked through Vincenzo's inclusion in the couple, we were able to suggest to the parents that their eldest child move out. Since he was about to start his military hitch anyway, he was taken in for several weeks by Anna's family. This measure instantly put Rosaria at ease. The treatment was facilitated by a fortunate circumstance: When the therapists decided to inform Signor Scalici about his serious clinical condition, he responded by immediately going on the wagon. This step led to his mental and physical recovery and a more favorable medical prognosis.

Given the presence of a social agency capable of a closer and more detailed monitoring of the conditions of the minors both at home and at school, we managed to conclude the evaluative phase of treatment by returning all the children, including Vincenzo, to the family after only four months of separation.

The treatment was regarded as concluded when the parents

and the therapists succeeded in shifting the exclusive focus of the session from Vincenzo and poor Anna, who as a pair had become the devil incarnate for the parents. Now they were able to talk about Rosaria and the four youngest children, who were becoming differentiated and recognizable, both in therapy sessions and at home.

This process of individuation in the children was also helped along by the foster family that had taken in the two youngest. In fact, the eagerness of the foster parents stimulated a healthy competition in the real parents: They wanted "possession" of their children, who at that moment represented a value to strive for rather than a burden.

The Abuse of the Scapegoat

We now come to the second category of family games that characterize abusive situations. These are the games in which the abuse victim actively participates in maintaining the pathogenic game.

It is true that even in the first category of games—parental unfitness as a message—it is not correct to view the child exclusively as the recipient of communications from others and specifically only as the victim of abuse. We ought to reconsider the two cases outlined in Chapter II. In both instances, a handicapped child is the victim of mistreatment by a parent who is dissatisfied with inadequate affection from his or her spouse. No doubt, the two minors in question, one of whom was not even an only child, presented a factor predisposing them to abuse, that is, their handicap. The literature on abuse is very clear on this topic (Camblin, 1982; Kienbergen & Diamond, 1985). In systemic terms, a handicap constitutes information to which the other family members cannot help reacting (Cirillo & Sorrentino, 1986; Sorrentino, 1987). Thus, we can see that the child has to be viewed not merely as receiving messages but also as sending them. These messages are the inherent distinction of the handicap and the resulting need for rehabilitation. But this does not mean that the child is considered a "strategist," i.e., the intentional sender of messages drawn from a gamut of possibilities. She performs that function in the second category of games, which we define as scapegoat games.

The Scapegoated Chick

Very often, the child who assumes the role of scapegoat—and hence is the sole victim of abuse or else receives the lion's share of it—maintains ties to several members of the extended family. Sometimes, he is the child of only one of the spouses, for which reason he has been raised by grandparents for a certain period of time. Let us describe a paradigmatic example.

Matteo, nine years of age, came to school with a bleeding gash in his scalp and various bruises on his body. He was instantly removed from his home, where he lived with his father, his father's companion, and the couple's two children, five and two years old. As in fairy tales, it appears as if the wicked stepmother loved her own children and beat her stepson, who received support and comfort only from his paternal grandmother. The reality, of course, was far more complex.

Matteo's father, Luigi, was living alone with his mother, a widow, until the day he brought home a girl, Ornella, whom he had impregnated. Ornella was very beautiful and very free, unlike Luigi, who was timid and clumsy. His mother opposed what she considered a shotgun wedding (which nevertheless took place) because she felt that Ornella was trying to fob off someone else's child on Luigi. Still, the young couple and their baby, Matteo, moved into two rooms in the grandmother's apartment. Naturally, the marriage collapsed within a year because of the violent fighting between Ornella and her mother-in-law—a discord that was exacerbated by Luigi's wishy-washy behavior. Ornella vanished; when she returned one week later, saying she had found lodgings elsewhere and wanted to pick up her child, the grandmother refused to hand him over.

Ornella gave up; she would then drop by sporadically to see the baby. During these visits, she was accompanied by several men who were supposed to intimidate her mother-in-law. But then one day, after being bullied by her mother-in-law, Ornella disappeared for good.

Three years later, Luigi began a relationship with Sandra, a strong-willed woman; they then settled down together in her village, several miles from his mother's home. His mother likewise opposed this second relationship and made it clear that she would never give up Matteo. Initially, Sandra knuckled under, doing her best to strengthen her relationship with Luigi and get him away from his mother's influence. But after the birth of their first child, a girl, Sandra tried again, telling Luigi that she wanted to take in Matteo. This was the only way that she could feel legitimized in all respects, both toward her mother-in-law and toward Ornella—who was still Luigi's legal wife and who occasionally ran into him on the streets of their village. Hemming and hawing, unable to make up his mind, Luigi asked Matteo (who was four years old!) what he wanted to do. Reaching a hard-fought compromise, they agreed to let Matteo spend his vacations during the next few years with Luigi's new family. After the birth of her second daughter, Sandra finally won, and Matteo, now seven years of age, came to live, more or less permanently, with his father and his stepmother. His grandmother, who was growing old, put up less resistance, partly because the boy was unruly and difficult to manage.

We can thus imagine that Matteo had very confused emotions when he left his grandmother. First of all, he felt guilty for abandoning her; furthermore, she had warned him against his stepmother, hinting that he would be mistreated there and would play second fiddle to his little half-sisters. In addition, although looking forward to living in a "real" family, he was simultaneously anxious and fearful.

Luigi, who had to reassure his son and help him to become

part of the family, was similarly unwilling to write off his mother and commit himself completely to his live-in companion. He put the boy in Sandra's care but missed no opportunity to come between them, almost fearing that she might be too harsh with Matteo. The boy, for his part, quickly tested his father and his stepmother: Whenever Sandra scolded and punished him, Luigi would instantly protect and defend him. Moreover, as if to make up for the unhappiness he had caused his son, Luigi offered to let the boy spend several vacation days with his grandmother. The grandmother obviously helped to fan the flames. With her, Matteo felt comforted and supported, but also excluded, indeed exiled from his father's home.

Over the next two years, Matteo became more and more uncontrollable. Even his grandmother, amid sighs and recriminations about how the boy had been treated, declared that she no longer wished to look after him. At this point, the abuse episode exploded, as Sandra's desperate attempt to exercise her own authority over the child and to strike back at the husband who refused to side with her.

When Matteo was removed from their home (and put up at our Center), the family was likewise taken in charge. During the evaluation meetings, the first of which included the grandmother, we succeeded in reconstructing the game described above. This enabled us to furnish the judge with a highly detailed evaluation of the family crisis, to suggest that the court allow Matteo to return home after three months at the Center, while the family began a real therapy. This treatment centered on Luigi's reluctance to "put himself in Sandra's hands" and on her relations with her own family, which were far more camouflaged than Luigi's blatant dependence on his mother. The therapy concluded six months later when Luigi began divorce proceedings against Ornella; this was his first step toward marrying Sandra.

One year after the termination of therapy, on the basis of the report made by the social service, which kept constant watch over Matteo's situation, the judge officially closed the file after a last meeting with Luigi and Sandra, the district social worker, and a member of our Center.

In our opinion, this case lucidly exemplifies how the game that leads to mistreatment is partially kept up by the child himself. Naturally, this does not mean that he is an accomplice in the abuse: He is, and he remains, a victim of abuse. Still, he has become a victim somewhat through his own strategies—partly because of unconscious choices, partly because of understandable motives, which are, however, erroneous, in that the child was hoping for entirely different results. Matteo, instigated by his grandmother, continued to emphasize how "different" he was, refusing to form any bond whatsoever with his stepmother. He had another "mamma" (she was, among other things, more beautiful than his stepmother, and he knew that he was her spitting image). In addition, the person who acted as his mother was his grandmother and certainly not the stranger living with his father!

It is easy to imagine that the game could have taken an entirely different course if Matteo had let himself be conquered by his "new mamma." He could perhaps have played the poor orphan boy who has never known his mother, thereby competing with his half-sisters for his stepmother's attention. Naturally, in order to pursue this tactic, he would have needed a father who did not use him as an instrument for his own vacillation, staying at a safe distance from his mother and from his companion alike (both of whom he seemed to fear profoundly). This cogently demonstrates the interconnections among the strategies of all the players, in a vortex of reciprocal influences in which not even the strategy adopted by Matteo can be underrated.

The Forecast of Incest

The game of "scapegoated chick" appears in several variants. The most significant type of situation is the one in which a man and his stepdaughter are ineluctably thrust toward one another by a forecast of incest, which is conjured up by everyone, including the participants. The following case illustrates this game.

Barbara came to the social worker and, amid profound reluctance and allusions that were instantly taken back, she complained about the pathological relationship that had developed between her husband and her 14-year-old daughter Annarosa. She had managed to explicitly confirm their relationship upon returning from the hospital, where she had been recovering from an abortion. Barbara asked for, and obtained, the removal of her daughter to a boarding school. Our Center was then assigned the task of evaluating the overall family situation.

Our first session included Annarosa; her mother, Barbara, who was only 14 years older than her daughter; Ugo, Barbara's husband, who had legally recognized Annarosa as his daughter at the time of his marriage, when the girl was two years old; and the couple's other five children. Barbara's and Ugo's families of origin, although highly significant, were not invited because they lived too far away and were impeded by problems of health and domestic organization.

This meeting laboriously brought Barbara's dramatic background to light. She had begun working when she was nine years old, and she had been impregnated by her boss when she was 13. Forty days after giving birth, she went back to work while her mother looked after her little girl. No charges were brought against her seducer, who continued to be received in the home of Barbara's parents. When Barbara married Ugo, who was from the same village, her mother refused to return the baby girl, even though Ugo had given her his own name. As a result, Annarosa believed that Barbara was her sister, and it was only when the child turned nine that she went to live with her parents and her half-siblings, of whom there were now three. Their home was a long way from the provincial village where she had been living.

In taking her back, Barbara had made a choice about which she was not completely secure. On the one hand, she did not wish to be unjust toward her daughter, since she was raising her later children; on the other hand, she was very fearful that Ugo might not like Annarosa because she was not his own child. However, something more hidden was gnawing at Barbara: Her mother's hints about what could happen if "you put the straw near the fire" made the young woman extremely apprehensive about the possible consequences. Ugo, for his part, did his best to make Annarosa feel at home, since he wanted to show his wife that he would not distinguish between his own children and her daughter. Ugo was a cheerful man with a sense of humor, and, during his brief moments at home, he would put the children on his lap and play with them. Barbara was glad to have them off her hands after taking care of them all day long. Annarosa, having lived in an all-female home (tormented by the physical and mental problems of Barbara's two sisters) was very attracted to her adoptive father, whom she barely knew.

Imperceptibly, the atmosphere in her new home changed within the space of a year. During the day, Annarosa fretted and responded nastily to her mother, who wanted her to help with the chores and the children (a new baby had recently joined them); in the evening, however, Annarosa was transformed, laughing nonstop with Ugo. Barbara began feeling jealous and was haunted more and more frequently by her mother's words, which she never managed to forget. Now, Barbara gradually became more cantankerous and ill-humored with both her daughter and her husband, at whom she aimed vague rebukes. Annarosa was quickly viewed by all as the third adult in the house and, before she even turned 13, she "stuck her nose" into discussions about their finances, which were disorderly, partly because the couple had had a sixth child.

In her sexual intimacy with Ugo and her continual pregnancies, Barbara was probably looking for a signal of her privileged bond with her husband, a bond that would differentiate her from her daughter. By now, however, she wanted to "test" her husband. When Annarosa complained about the cold (the house had no heat source) and a stomachache, her mother let the girl take her place in the matrimonial bed while she herself slept on the kitchen sofa. Little by little, Annarosa appeared more and more triumphant and brazen, never stifling her adolescent exuberance; at the same time, Barbara isolated herself more and more, neglecting her children and going on long crying jags by the stove. When she decided to interrupt her next pregnancy, Ugo was uninterested and did not even accompany her to the hospital. Returning home, she found the apartment topsy-turvy; her daughter was on her husband's lap, and they were playing cards with a female friend. Spying on them, she caught Ugo reaching under Annarosa's skirt. Notifying the social worker, though necessary for the protection of Annarosa, was viewed by Barbara as an act of revenge upon her husband.

In working with the family, we had an extremely difficult time revealing Ugo's strategies in the family game, while it was relatively easy to illuminate the roles of Barbara, Annarosa, and the grandmother. Ugo displayed the blithe ingenuousness of someone who has simply replied to the moves of others, always playing the responsive part: Barbara kept growing more and more cantankerous and unfathomable, weeping for no reason; Annarosa was always cheerful, affectionate, she seemed to want to console Ugo for his wife's nasty character. He, however, claimed that he "never did anything wrong" with Annarosa. It was thus an uphill battle to piece together and reconstruct the other side of the coin: Ugo's rancor toward Barbara for never allowing him to act as Annarosa's father because she was not his child; his annoyance at the airs put on by the bossy little girl, with whom he was unable to assert himself. Barbara's accusations against her husband ("He let Annarosa insult me, and he never defended me.") finally evoked a retort from Ugo: "You allowed the girl to walk all over me." Gradually, the spouses realized that they had jointly contributed to casting Annarosa in the part of the "real" mistress of the house, allowing her to provoke both mother and father, without ever giving her the signal that would put her back in her filial position.

The judge then suggested that Annarosa spend Sundays at home so that they might attempt to reorganize the family roles. The ongoing treatment of the couple aimed at including the girl in the group of children, cementing the marital relationship through the therapeutic device of placing both parents on the same level, as being jointly responsible for the trauma that they had inflicted upon their daughter. Nevertheless, an important part of the therapy would be devoted to inducing Ugo to undergo a radical self-critique. For an authentic reconciliation with both his wife and Annarosa, Ugo would have to gain (and declare) the awareness that he had struck at the girl's mental and physical integrity and at the couple's marital bond—moves that were far more devastating than Barbara's provocations.[2]

The Risks of Being One Parent's Defender

There is another family constellation in which child abuse involves active participation by the victim: in such a case, the parents are trapped in a violent dead-end conflict that induces the children to join in by siding with the parent who seems weaker to them. When allying herself with the parent whom she perceives as the victim (but

2. This volume will not be dealing with the theme of incest, which, however, forms the subject of a work edited by Marinella Malacrea and Alessandro Vassalli (1990); one of their goals is to illustrate the CBM experiences in this domain. Here, we only wish to remind the reader that the games underlying the phenomenon of incest are quite specific. In this book, we presented a typology of the incestuous family (Cirillo, Di Blasio, Malacrea, & Vassalli, 1990); for simplicity's sake, we limited our analysis to the father/mother/daughter triad. To emphasize the daughter's active part in the game (a difficult aspect to grasp in our linear mentality, which inexorably separates victim from victimizer), we named each variant after the daughter's specific role. We thus categorized incestuous families with a "pitied" daughter, a "fascinated" daughter, or a "treacherous" daughter. An acute analysis of the functionings of an incestuous triad can be found in the works of Furniss (1983, 1984, 1985), which also contain a wealth of valuable and effective information.

who actually helps to provoke the conflict, albeit more covertly), the child often becomes the target of aggression transferred from the seemingly stronger parent. In this way, the child detonates the explosion of abuse. Here is a particularly good example:

Agata arrived with her son Claudio to request help from a nun, who provided assistance to families in a poor section of the city. Agata explained that her husband, Nicola, beat her violently because she opposed Nicola's homosexual relationship with a 20-year-old boy whom he wanted to put up in their home. The weeping mother explained that her husband had been repeatedly sentenced for theft, fencing stolen goods, and passing bad checks. As a result, he had lost his job as a brick-layer and now spent all his time at a bar and in a gaming room. Agata did part-time domestic work, supplementing her wages with welfare payments. Aside from Claudio, she also had a daughter named Rosalba; the girl was being cared for by a great-aunt who resided in the vicinity. Agata had brought her ten-year-old son with her because he understood and helped her. For this reason, the father was often upset with Claudio too and beat the boy when he tried to defend his mother.

The next day, the nun accompanied Agata to the welfare office, which reported the situation to the Juvenile Court. When the judge summoned the parents, Agata denied everything. But then, a short time later, Claudio's school filed a report stating that the boy showed black-and-blue marks that were obvious signs of beatings. The judge then decided to order an inquiry, which also involved the participation of our Center.

Despite countless difficulties, we succeeded, on the basis of the family's history, in ferreting out the specific nature of the provocations between husband and wife, beyond Claudio's obvious attribution of the roles of victim and persecutor.

Agata had met Nicola in Milan; she had moved here from the south after breaking off with her mother and was living with an aunt. Her father had been serving a prison sentence for many years. Nicola had grown up in an orphanage, where he had received some education; he had lived alone for several years. Agata and Nicola got married, but, one week after the wedding, Agata took their meager nest egg and returned to her mother's home without informing her husband. He followed her, and Agata claimed she wanted to move back to the village to be near her family. Nicola reluctantly agreed; but several years later, he went back north to look for a job, and Agata agreed to follow him, leaving little Claudio in her mother's care. This ballet dragged on for years: Every chance she got, Agata would run back to her mother, and it took heaven and earth for Nicola to talk her into coming home. On the other hand, when Agata was in Milan, she exhibited her attachment to his aunt, even turning the latter against Nicola. He, for his part, committed far more serious provocations: run-ins with the law, unemployment, beatings, and finally his homosexual betrayal. Her husband's conduct obviously kept forcing Agata to seek refuge more and more often with her mother. It was precisely Nicola's mishaps that won him a special place in Agata's heart, because, as a girl, she felt neglected in comparison with her brothers; her suffering won her mother's attention. And it was equally clear that Agata's escapes made Nicola more and more furious and reactive.

However, the children, Claudio and Rosalba, naturally failed to see the circularity of this interaction. It was far easier for them to notice their father's wrongdoings (which were obvious and constantly underscored by Agata's complaints) than their mother's misdeeds, especially because they really liked their grandmother and their great-aunt for lavishing attention on them. The position of Claudio, the highly intelligent and sensitive male firstborn, made him the most likely candidate for his role as his mother's defender and his father's rival. Indeed, Agata kept involving the boy in her conflicts with her husband, and Claudio gladly volunteered to console her, while Rosalba remained in the protected position as younger daughter, who sided with no one and very often simply played at her aunt's home.

Once we exposed the game and obtained a court order to try and terminate it, our therapy aimed chiefly at undermining Claudio's pathogenic role within the couple.

The spouses were united in the joint task of being Claudio's parents. As such, they were confronted with the fact that a heavy burden was weighing down the future of their son, on whose precocious intelligence they had so sharply focused. In fact, the boy, trapped in his absurd role as the third adult in the family, tended to assume "grown-up" behavior even outside the house, which made him unbearable to his companions and his teachers. Furthermore, he had learned how to take advantage of his difficult situation, dodging his scholastic responsibilities by playing the victim and flaunting his dismal family situation. The effort to have Claudio's parents cooperate in regard to a protective intervention for their son was successful, enabling us to work indirectly on the underlying marital conflict.

Incidentally, we must observe that the treatment of a conflict cannot be limited to exploring each participant's reasons for dissatisfaction. The therapists should also focus on the specific actions of the two spouses. In the example presented above, Agata resorts to passivity and "underground" manipulation, and Nicola to violence and crime. The origins of these different strategies are to be found either in the respective learning contexts or in the game of mutual influence. In regard to the peculiar interactive styles of these spouses, their encounter has obviously led to accentuating these styles rather than correcting them!

The Defender of the Absent Party

An extremely frequent variant of this game, in which the child sides with the parent who seems weaker, is to be found when the spouses separate. According to the literature on this subject, abuse cases occur more often in families having only one parent, generally the mother (Sack, Mason, & Higgins, 1985). A dyadic interpretation of the phenomenon takes several factors into account: the tension and over-burdening of the single mother who has to perform her parental tasks alone, the depression caused by the solitude in which she lives, and the lack of support at moments of stress.

Nevertheless, we must widen our field of observation to include a third party, the father—if only to prevent him from playing an active part in the game. In cases of "parental unfitness as a message," this same expansion of the field helped us to discover a "traitor" who enjoys life and is completely irresponsible about the children he has fathered. Here, by broadening the field, we can unearth a very different web of relationships.

We often find that the father maintains contact with the children—directly or through intermediaries like the grandmother or the children's aunt. In this way, the children become aware of the miserable conditions in which their father lives. He may be staying in objectively unpleasant surroundings (a public shelter, a rooming house, his place of work) and yet he has been forced to leave home. It is likely that in the eyes of the children it seems that he has been "kicked out of his home" by their mother. In this atmosphere of mutual accusations—an atmosphere typical of a conflict-ridden separation—the father feeds the children a negative image of the mother. He depicts her as the "villain" who prevents them from being with him, seeing him, having meals with him, getting a good-night kiss from him, and so forth. On the one hand, the child feels compassion with the lonesome father, who is forced to roam the world; on the other hand, he becomes resentful toward his mother for depriving him of his father.

Naturally, in this situation, the child is also utterly unaware of the provocative character of the father's actions. For example, the father spends years in a public shelter rather than looking for an apartment; he drinks to "forget" and to console himself for his difficult situation. These moves aim at stirring pity and/or guilt in his ex-wife. Other moves, such as entering into a relationship with a blatantly inappropriate person (an older woman, an addict, a prostitute) may have two goals: to make the ex-wife jealous and to show her how deep she has let him "sink."

Furthermore, in the traditional system of joint custody, a child spends workdays with her mother and pleasure time with her father. This division encourages the child to idealize the good and permissive father and to resent the demanding, impatient, authoritarian mother. In this framework, the child's insubordination almost inevitably leads to the mother's abusing her. The child lives with her mother, but nurtures a grudge toward her—filled as she is with pity and compassion for her "lost" father and taking his side completely. Furthermore, whenever she spends time with her father, the child is sharply, albeit not explicitly, instigated against the mother.

Meanwhile, the mother, who is the sole provider for the child, begins to feel the burden of her sacrifices. She is conscious of the wrongs inflicted on her by her ex-husband, who has never helped her raise the child. And she is equally conscious of the wrongs that she will continue to suffer, if he—as is so often the case—fails to contribute child support. For this reason, the child's disobedience and trouble-making, her constant defense of her father, her complicity with him in trying to get her mother to let her ex-husband return while she strenuously tries to prevent his interference—all these things strike the mother as an unfair and bitter betrayal. The ultimate outcome is abuse, which frequently explodes when she falls prey to depression—and even alcoholism.

Obviously, we can attempt to resolve this type of predicament by supporting the single mother, but only after properly reconstructing the complexity of the game and illustrating it clearly to the father and the child. In this connection, we have several goals. We want to make it harder for the man to continue his instigative and seductive moves, which are now exposed to everyone. Likewise, we want to make it more difficult for the child to act as the father's unwitting instrument, and we want to guide the child toward understanding the problems her mother has to cope with.

The Child in the Abuse Process

All these descriptions of family games, in their dynamic complexity, may transmit an overly rigid vision of the roles played by the individual participants. One might erroneously conclude that they are playing the same roles now as in the past.

Indeed, when the family presents itself for our observation, the temporal plane that can be explored is limited compared with the far longer and more extensive period in which the tangle of relationships developed, coalescing in the specific family game. Whatever we cannot observe directly we try to reconstruct from verbalizations by the participants or other members of the extended family. This is one of the reasons why these members take part in the sessions: to help bring out facts that the individual memories have reinterpreted personally or events that they have preferred to suppress.

However, even our reconstruction is geared to the present. It is oriented toward completing our explanation of what is happening now, and it enables us to describe the current game in such a way that the past, with its relevant role, contributes to revealing the complexity of the present dynamics. Thus, the description may disclose a game that seems stable, fixed, and structured according to organizational rules and parameters as valid today as in the past. Yet we know that a group is temporally organized through trials and errors, which, occasionally following principles of discontinuity rather than continuity, gradually produce the unfortunate relational tangles that we are given to observe. A description of such phenomena cannot always keep track of the progression of events (diachronic longitudinal dimension) and the things that are occurring at present (synchronic transversal dimension).

For this reason, we like to amplify the description of games by offering several comments—essentially about the position of the child in the process that supports the abuse. These comments are more useful in stimulating subsequent investigations than as solid and definitive insights. They are based on a diachronic perspective that illuminates the history of the abuse and its various stages.[3] The referential

3. The reflections in this part are reworkings of a paper, "Emotional reactions in abused children," presented by Paola Di Blasio at the 21st International Congress of Applied Psychology, Jerusalem, 1986.

diagram we have used was the more complex one developed by Selvini Palazzoli et al. (1989) for analyzing psychotic games. In their diagram, the authors identified a process involving six stages. Analogous to this model and on the basis of our own observations of family violence, we have delineated several phases that characterize the dynamics of an abusive family. Our focus is limited to physical violence because this is the only area in which we have observed enough cases to make valid generalizations. It would be inappropriate to apply these inferences to situations of neglect or sexual abuse, which go through their own stages of evolution, overlapping only partly with the sequence that characterizes physical maltreatment.

First Stage: The Couple's Conflict

In the first stage, the family in which child abuse develops presents an explicit spousal conflict marked by one partner's constant and systematic opposition to the other. It appears to be a no-win struggle punctuated by more or less short break-ups, constant threats of separation, and subsequent reconciliations. In other words, the marriage is subject to perpetual fluctuations, and the spouses find it is as impossible to stay together as it is to break up.

One could think that the disagreeable family conditions, the economic dependency of one spouse (usually the wife), and the bad housing circumstances play a major part in discouraging the termination of what is nevertheless an unsatisfactory marriage. Yet we know that such factors, although important, do not motivate the perpetuation of the marriage, even if, by virtue of their objective character, they become pretexts for justifying a lack of any change. Quite the contrary: The conflict endures precisely because each spouse keeps hoping to change the other and get him or her to surrender in some way.

In such a situation, the parents may eventually rigidify into two distinct roles, whereby one spouse constantly seems to be enduring the other's impositions and decisions, while the second partner appears to be playing a superior and dominating role. Simply put, two positions are defined: that of a seemingly passive victim and that of a seemingly active dominator. More precisely, when we speak of a victim, we mean – in accordance with Selvini Palazzoli et al. (1989) – a position that only seems inactive, because this individual is actually playing the covert role of a "passive instigator." Similarly, with the term "dominator," we are referring to what only appears to be the dominant position in the relationship. In fact, this person is using the blatant moves of active instigation.[4]

During this phase, the child is still a mere spectator of the conflict, even though he or she may express disturbance through sporadic reactions of anxiety and irritability.

4. We need a clarification at this point, because we are focusing on a spousal conflict, which, in this first stage, can lead to spousal violence even if the abuse is not yet directed at the child. Such behavior is rightfully stigmatized by society and, in more severe cases, punished by the law. It is fair to side with the victim of physical violence, since he or she may not be able to avoid it, and we have no intention of denying the validity of this evaluation. Nevertheless, if we want to understand the problem from the less simplistic psychological perspective of common sense, we are duty-bound to analyze the emotional impulses of the person who finds himself in a disadvantageous and subordinate position. According to our observations, the individual in this position is persuaded that the lack of his or her own space for autonomy and action is specifically the partner's fault. Sustained by this conviction, one can obstinately try to modify the partner's character and conduct, never explicitly, but through implicit strategies of boycott, passive resistance, making the partner feel guilty, and casting oneself in the role of victim. Yet these modalities trigger the aggressive and violent behavior that the victim wishes to eliminate. The failure of that strategy, rather than discouraging the persecutor, intensifies his feelings of impotence, dim rage, and vindictiveness, which all combine to mobilize reactions of passive provocation. It must be made clear that the definition of "passive provoker" (and, conversely, "active provoker") is not a value judgment, nor does it assign guilt; rather, it expresses a position within the specific processes of the family game that we are dealing with. Obviously, not every troubled couple is made up of an aggressive husband and a subordinate and seemingly passive wife. In our case work, we also find, albeit less frequently, couples in which the wife seems dominant (she has a career, she earns a living, and has social relationships); her behavior arouses her husband's jealousy, anger, and possessiveness. In this case, the term "victim," or better, "passive provoker," is applied to the husband, who is psychologically incapable of reacting or of modifying himself, since he is constantly frustrated by his wife's behavior and subtly resolves to get the better of her, even instigating their child against her, if only to demonstrate to her that she has failed as a mother.

Second Stage: The Children Take Sides

In the second stage of the persistent conflict, the children are impelled to get involved and take sides with either parent. Unaware of the complexity and circularity of the couple's relationship, the offspring ally themselves with the parent whom they view as weak and victimized. Moved by feelings of empathy, they approach and hope to console the parent who manifests disturbance and suffering in a way that they are able to understand. This type of emotional involvement can be observed even in three- or four-year-olds. Furthermore, as investigations of empathy have shown, even children younger than that are sensitive to other people's discomfort and suffering, which they, the children, somehow try to alleviate in order to keep from feeling pain.

The works of numerous researchers — Radke-Yarrow and Zahn Waxler (1976), Rheingold et al. (1976), Sagi and Hoffman (1976), Hoffman (1979, 1982), Hinchey and Gavelek (1982) — disprove the stereotype of the child who is insensitive to complaints and expressions of suffering. Indeed, even during their first few years, children begin to manifest an empathic ability — presaging altruistic behavior — which allows them to recognize pain and disturbance in others. Through a kind of emotional "contagion," they are able to share these sufferings and to marshal attentive and behavioral responses aimed at assuaging them. In our case, the child's propensity for getting close to a parent in order to alleviate his suffering is welcomed by that parent, who unwittingly encourages this inversion of roles. As emphasized by De Lozier (1982) and Masson (1981), the parent may be impelled to do so by analogous childhood experiences: He or she may have once taken the same position of consoling a parent. In other words, the adult looks for support, solace, and comfort from the child, confiding her marital disappointments, expressing dissatisfaction with the partner, and expecting a relationship of complicity with the child. Thus, the foundations are laid for a type of relationship characterized by the presence of a more or less explicit alliance between members of two different generations (parent and child) against a third person (the other spouse).[5] Obviously, if the couple's conflict is resolved through a positive change, then there is a strong likelihood that the phenomena described above will tend to gradually disappear, so that no coalition is formed. And even if the conflict is not resolved through reconciliation, it may be modified by other solutions. For example, one partner may eventually prefer to leave the other, because she is convinced that she can bank on the child's help in establishing a solid emotional relationship.

In other cases, however, the alliance with the child can be used to produce one of those well-known fictitious separations, which typically feature the use of the child as a pawn in negotiating a different kind of relationship with the partner. An example of such cases can be the one in which the wife reveals the husband's violence toward her, asks for protection with the child, and says that she wants a separation—in the hope that her threat will induce the man to alter his behavior. If all goes well, this move can result in a new discussion of the family rules. But more often than not, the wife's words remain a mere threat, unsupported by any concrete decision to stipulate specific demands of the partner. In such cases, the reconciliation is swift, the woman retracts the accusations she has leveled at her husband, and any admission of problems is put on hold. Since moves of this type can recur over and over again, the family game remains unchanged.

Third Stage: The Active Coalition of the Child

Next comes a third stage, in which the child, who has taken sides with one of the parents, starts to act out her own hostility toward

5. The concept of coalition became part of the explanatory criteria used by family therapists when Haley (1963, 1971) defined the "denied coalition" as a modality of a pathological relationship inherent in so-called "perverse triangles." The subsequent clinical observations, confirming the validity of this interpretational parameter, have failed to indicate further versions—for instance, the simple coalition and the cross coalition. This concept was extended to the institutional framework by the Selvini Palazzoli group to illustrate a possible modality of the relationship between the consulting psychologist and the client/organization (Di Blasio, 1987).

the other parent. In the more or less frequent conflicts, the child, no longer a mere spectator, operates in defense of one parent against the other. The child openly expresses her own feelings of fear, rage, rancor, and hostility, which are accompanied by antagonistic and rebellious behavior, such as refusing to eat, to get up in the morning, to wash, to get dressed, to go to bed, to switch off the TV, to do homework. During this phase, the child acts combative toward only one parent.

This web of emotional and behavioral reactions is quite selective, that is, it is leveled specifically at the parent whom we have called the "active instigator," and who, in the eyes of the child, seems victorious and dominating. It must be noted that the child's expressions of rage and aggression are actively inflamed by the signals she receives from the "victim."

The provocation takes place on the fertile terrain of negative emotions that the child already feels toward the active instigator's rigid, irascible, and authoritarian behavior, which is often expressed in this parent's direct relationship with the child.

Outside the family circle, the child gradually becomes more and more irritable, anxious, and distracted, while almost never responding with rage or aggression.

If the conflict persists, the child tends to adopt a stable battery of aggressive responses, which she subsequently utilizes even outside the family.

Fourth Stage: Exploiting the Child's Responses

In the fourth and final stage—which we can define as an exploitation of the child's responses—the family game becomes more complex because the child in turn assumes the position of the active instigator of mistreatment.

What normally happens? The parents are unable to interpret the child's emotional and behavioral responses as signals directly tied to the couple's conflict. They read the rage and aggressiveness as signs of spite, rebellion, and disobedience, which are then drastically punished. The child's reactions are used by the parents to hurl mutual accusations of incompetence and unfitness at each other.

The couple's conflict begins to encompass problems of upbringing, and the parents assume stereotypical roles. Trying to control the child's behavior, one parent becomes excessively permissive and the other excessively authoritarian. Indeed, their competitiveness becomes provocative as they vie to show who is the better parent, whereby each almost automatically disqualifies the other's child-rearing methods. At this point, the child feels betrayed and has a frustrating sense of being a mere weapon in the parents' struggle, so that she winds up hating the two of them and expressing rage, hostility, and aggressiveness toward father *and* mother indiscriminately. In the course of this behavior, the child becomes both the victim and instigator of violence. She is transformed into an active protagonist, perpetuating the game that underlies the abuse.

The Child's Cognitive Development and Perception of the Parental Conflict

It would be interesting to gain a better grasp of the specific factors of maturation and experience that help to stabilize the child's emotional reactions. In the length of our observations, the sixth and seventh year constitute a particularly critical time, when the child begins to assume a role of active aggressor first inside and then outside the family. We can attempt to explain this process by integrating our previous observations with several remarks on the development of cognitive and moral faculties during childhood.

From the classical studies of Piaget (1947/76) and Kohlberg (1976), we know that, prior to the age of six, a child sets great store in obeying and respecting rules only because they derive from adult authority. The child will therefore tend to view as just both the standards maintained by that authority and the behavior that can avoid incurring punishment.

In the family set-up that we have described, the child of that age does not overtly buck the authority of the parent whom she regards as dishonest. This reluctance is due both to fear of punishment and to a basic inability to place value judgments of just or unjust in terms of personal criteria. As we have said, the child feels emotionally close to the parent whom she considers a victim; the child develops hostile feelings toward the other parent and tends to picture herself as an avenger applying the law of retaliation. However, toward the age of six or seven, the child acquires standards of judgment based on a notion of distributive justice. Above all, the child now develops a capacity for judging other people's intentions and putting herself in their shoes (role-taking). These abilities give the child a new view of familial relationships. Aside from reacting empathically to the "victim's" suffering, the child now seeks to understand and interpret the latter's intentions. The desires for revenge and reprisal that animate the "victim" are perceived by the child as just reasons for the "victim's" conflict with the spouse. The child is certainly in no position to understand, in logical or in relational terms, the interconnections in the parental relationship. Dominated by a schema of simple and linear interpretation, the child feels that the most blatant wrongdoing, even that of an adult, has to be punished so that the conditions of equity and justice can be restored. The child will therefore begin to rebel in hopes of punishing the culprit and obtaining the gratitude of the parent whom the child is defending. But these hopes are dashed, the conflict between the parents grows more and more bitter, and the child's behavior is viewed negatively even by the parent to whom she is emotionally closer. Viewing these developments as a betrayal, the child feels that she is being treated unfairly, bullied — this time by the "victim." The child therefore rebels both inside and outside the family. To clarify these processes, Table 1 sums up the child's reactions in the evolution of the family game.

TABLE 1: *Evolution of the family game, and the child's reactions.*

Phases of the family game	Child's reactions
Stage 1: Spousal conflict	Anxiety, irritability
Stage 2: Child takes sides	Anxiety, fear, empathy
Stage 3: Active coalition	Rage, aggression
Stage 4: Child exploited as tool	Rage, aggression, hostility outside family

Feelings of Abandonment in the Abusive Parent

So far, we have tried to put ourselves in the child's shoes by analyzing the tangle of overwhelming emotions that impel the child to enter the fray, give up his passive role, and become furiously aggressive and show symptomatic behavior.

We will now put ourselves in the abusive parent's shoes and analyze one of his motives for inflicting physical violence on the child—a conduct that is certainly different from the verbal bullying or (occasional or systematic) physical violence inflicted by one spouse on the other. Our research has shown us that such child abuse is rooted in a fear of loss and abandonment. Psychoanalytical studies underscore the fact that abusive parents tend to react to separation with anxiety and rage (De Lozier, 1982). Bowlby's hypothesis, based on a psychoanalytical model that is strongly influenced by ethology, takes off from the interpretation of functional rage and arrives at an explanation of dysfunctional rage. If expressed at the right time and place, says Bowlby, such rage operates as a response that can maintain and protect the individual's specific and vital relations, e.g., with a sexual partner, with his or her parents, or with his or her child. "A great deal of the maladaptive violence met with in families can be understood as the distorted and exaggerated versions of behavior that is potentially functional, especially attachment behavior on the one hand and caregiving behavior on the other" (Bowlby, 1984, p. 12). Thus, from this perspective, violence against a child is an inadequate way of manifesting the rage and anxiety produced by a fear of loss and separation. Observation of these parents reveal the presence of their extreme sensitivity "to any type of separation situation, even the most everyday and commonplace" (p. 15). And, as might be expected, this is true not only because these people actually experienced separation from their families of origin, but also because they repeatedly endured the threat of being abandoned by their own parents. This is a sign that "repeated threats to abandon are as pathogenic as actual separation and probably more so" (p. 16).

If we utilize these indications within our perspective, which is based on the concept of the family game, we can observe that abusive parents react with rage, anxiety, and hostility not only because of their past experiences, but also because they confusedly feel left out of the coalition that has been established between their partner and the child. This perception is vague and they are bewildered because of the very nature of the intergenerational coalition, which, as we have seen, cannot be clearly articulated. What the parent perceives comes solely from indirect analogical signals, that is, the ones linked to the child's conduct. The child's hostility, rebellion, and aggression toward the parent—actions that the spouse does nothing to contain or mitigate—are signals of a rejection, of a loss and separation, and also of an alliance and rapport from which the parent feels excluded and to which he therefore responds with rage.

The Chronic Degeneration of the Process

As we have seen, the child's responses (Gaensbauer & Sands, 1979; Martin & Rodeheffer, 1980) are the only possible and appropriate ones within the family milieu. For this reason, the child eventually tends to adopt them as stable strategies outside the family as well.

We have repeatedly emphasized that, in order to be effective, the psychological treatment of abuse must alter the position that each member occupies in the family game. All the members including the child, are equally prisoners of a dysfunctional game in which they cannot help playing an active role. Individual clinical therapy risks being partial and ineffective, above all during the initial phase of addressing the problem.

We have been able to verify that, in cases of acute mistreatment, the child's responses, independent of his age, are not yet structured in a stable form and may therefore modify the family game. As is obvious, the structuring of a stable system of emotional responses necessitates a learning context that persists through time. An acute episode of maltreatment does not suffice in and of itself to cause a child to develop the complex emotional and behavioral configuration that we have described. In cases of chronic and repeated abuse, there are possibilities of recovery through treatment if the family game has not yet reached the fourth stage. On the other hand, once family relationships evolve according to the modalities of the fourth stage, family therapy by itself is often inadequate. The modification of emotional and behavioral responses would require simultaneous treatment in several areas of the child's life—school, peer group, parental relations, etc.—supplemented by individual psychotherapy.

VI | THERAPY IN THE MANDATED CONTEXT

The Relationship Between Therapy and Control: Maintaining Responsibility for a Case

THE NEXUS OF WORK IN mandated therapy is and remains the difficult relationship between help and control. The problem has been tackled repeatedly, and one approach is based on theoretical premises that are very close to ours (Bianchi & Rangone, 1985; Mastropaolo et al., 1985). This method usually involves a clean split between the therapeutic context and the context of control.

During the first few years, we too resorted to this formula. Different professionals, within two separate agencies, performed their diverse functions independently of each other: The psychologists at our Center did the therapy; the district social worker did the control. The integration between the two services was relative and casual; it involved a sporadic exchange of news and a unilateral effort by the social worker to reinforce the patients' commitment to psychotherapy.

Later on, we realized more and more clearly that therapy and control are actually two sides of the same coin, and that both are part of the larger context of protecting the child.[1] As we stated in Chapter IV, it is only toward this end that the family—which requires no other aid—is reached by the treatment. This process necessitates a precise report that describes the suffering and damage (and/or objectifiable risks) inflicted on the minor; and it is only on the basis of this report that we can track down the material for working with a family that denies and/or minimizes their problems. It is only through a regular contact with the social workers that the therapists can get hold of precise data indicating either the possible continuation of the problem or, vice versa, the scope and stability of the change. The therapeutic team cannot rely on help from the family, which may not be motivated to report any problems that persist or any crises that transpire between sessions. Quite the contrary: The therapeutic team can rely solely on accurate information gathered by the control team.

It follows that a split between therapy and control, aiming at complete mutual independence, strikes us as not only artificial but also doomed to failure. How are the therapists supposed to act if the clients abandon treatment? What material can we go by if the family states that every problem has been magically resolved? What good does it do for the therapists to appear before the judge but to hide behind client confidentiality and stick purely to formal aspects (such as whether the family members keep or ignore appointments) when this evaluation is done precisely for the judge as an investigation or assessment?

We recently worked out and formalized a different operative tactic. The first session in the therapeutic process serves chiefly to define the context, implicitly and explicitly. At this meeting, the family finds not only the team assigned to perform the diagnosis and any possible therapy, but also the district social service in charge of monitoring the case. The social worker briefs the team on the

---

1. This gradual awareness was encouraged by the concord between our approach and the acute reflections in Crivillé (1987). His work, too, advances from critique to the firm principle that a therapeutic role is incompatible with an authority role.

background of the case and on the reasons why the authorities were notified: He rereads the court order that has sent the family to our Center for evaluation, while also turning the minors over to the social agency. The social worker then follows the rest of the session from behind a one-way mirror, perhaps helping the psychologist and the family to reconstruct the problem. As a rule, the social worker does not attend later meetings. However, before each session, he calls up the Center colleague to relay information drawn from several sources: meetings with one or both parents, important telephone calls, data supplied on the minors by their respective residential homes or foster families, interference from relatives, contacts with the judge, and so on. Likewise, after each session, the diagnostic or therapeutic team reports to the social service, transmitting the gist of the session and the information received from the clients. If these telephone calls prove inadequate, the two services then get together physically.

Consistent with our basic statement of transparency toward both sides, we keep the family fully abreast of this close collaboration between the Center and the district services. This militates against any artificial polarizing between the "bad" caseworker, who has taken away the children, and the "good" therapist, who will do her best to restore them to the family. Such a dichotomy can be bridged if the therapist constantly and explicitly uses the information conveyed by her colleague, the district social worker. Naturally, the client should gradually realize that the therapist's use of these data is neither accusatory nor punitive. Should the client relapse into abusive or neglectful behavior, then, of course, the therapist must instantly notify the judge, who will take further measures to protect the minor. Otherwise, however, the therapist normally employs the material received from the social service to deepen her knowledge of the family game; the therapist's goal is to help the clients develop the game in a positive direction. As the clients gradually become more and more aware of the goal of their treatment, we witness a diminishing of their understandable reluctance to spontaneously report the problems and difficulties that they may have encountered between sessions.

The fact that the district social worker has not changed into a policeman is borne out by his possible interventions in support of the clients, whenever necessary. The caseworker sees them through the red tape involved in obtaining welfare, a new apartment, or a job; he facilitates their contacts with the children's schools, the institutions, and/or the foster families. In all these ways, the caseworker constantly demonstrates to the couple that he is helping them along the road to becoming fit parents. By so doing, the social service performs two tasks: It keeps track of the parents' progress as reported by the therapist, and it consolidates and stimulates this progress parallel with the therapy.

The results of diagnosis, therapy, and control are transmitted to the judge, who uses these reports as the basis for what he views as advisable decisions. This effectively places the contexts of both therapy and control in the wider and more important framework of the protection of the minor, which includes those contexts.

In our organizational model, our Center's social worker performs the complex task of integrating the family, the monitorial apparatus, and the diagnostic-therapeutic apparatus—a task that we define as "maintaining the responsibility for a case." After implementing the preliminary operations of setting our intervention and compiling the family chart, our social worker joins the supervising therapist behind the mirror. Besides attending every family session, the social worker, between sessions, has the job of integrating the needs dictated by the evolution of the diagnostic or therapeutic process with the necessities of shielding the minor. These necessities are expressed by the district service, the court, and the people and/or places housing the minors: the residential center, the institution, or the foster family. The social worker's job allows him to stay in charge of the family: He tries both to prevent the members from fleeing and to block their manipulators, to which the social workers and therapists would be bound to fall prey without mutual coordination. The Center's social worker also tries to avert or combat the dysfunctions that easily crop up in an often highly complex and intricate network of agencies: school, hospital, police, volunteers, social services, juvenile court, mental health services for adults and/or minors, etc.

Although complicated and difficult to organize and maintain, the integration of therapy and monitoring appears to be an indispensable requisite for a mandated case. In essence, these are two complementary functions that join forces in protecting the minor while helping the abusive family to recover. If we accept this principle of cooperation, we can more readily understand the experiences of a both fundamental and specialized district service. Take the Psychomedical and Pedagogical Unit of Lausanne, directed by Odette Masson: Here, the tasks of therapy and monitoring are implemented not only by the same agency, but by the same individuals! Our Center, being specialized, currently follows a different model: We perform diagnosis and therapy, while the district social service is mainly in charge of monitoring. However, as we have emphasized, these two functions are integrated as thoroughly as possible. (A pilot project has shown that nothing prevents both tasks from being rapidly assimilated and transferred in toto to the district service alone) (Soavi & Vianello, 1990).

Therapeutic Techniques: The Impossibility of Resorting to Paradoxes

During the early 1980s, when our team began working with abusive families, the family therapists in the Milan area were still making frequent use of the paradox method. As we all know, the counterparadoxical use, during the first session, of the prescription of the symptom (Selvini Palazzoli et al., 1984) had, among other things, the goal of reinforcing the family's commitment to therapy. That was the era of "systemic purism." In polar opposition to intrapsychic theories with a psychoanalytic orientation, the therapeutic categories were those of holistic psychology, which, within the system, noted the presence of factions, coalitions, and individual moves. From this perspective, any request for therapy was read in terms of a compromise between two coexisting but opposing tendencies: the homeostatic urge and the urge to change. These tendencies, initially used as explanatory constructs, were eventually almost reified by family therapists as attributes that were actually functioning in the system, which was virtually personified in its turn.

It was therefore claimed that the request for family therapy, an action that seemed to point toward change, was actually a homeostatic move on the part of the family, which felt that its internal equilibrium was threatened by the symptom of the designated patient. Thus, the family was asking for help in changing (that is, eliminating the symptom) in order to *avoid* changing (that is, in order to leave its own organization of relationships intact). From this perspective, it seemed quite logical for the therapist, at the first session, to go along with the prevalent homeostatic tendencies in the family and to prescribe the continuation of the symptom. Indeed, it was felt that any too blatantly antihomeostatic prescription for change would cause the family to become obstinately defensive and drop out of therapy.

These comments can also apply, at first sight, to the context of mandated therapy. The abusive family also has a powerful resistance to change—so powerful that the members refuse to seek help! As a result, any alliance with their homeostatic tendencies could prove to be a particularly shrewd strategy. But unfortunately, given the context, an agency cannot possibly formulate a prescription for the specific symptom—that is, order the culprits to keep beating their children for the sake of the family's unity and well-being!

Obviously, such an intervention would thoroughly clash with all the contextual markers—the nature of the treatment center, the mandate actions of the court, etc. Instead of sounding provocative, as an effective paradox is meant to be, such an intervention would, at the very least, seem absurd, if not downright criminal.

Furthermore, even apart from the specific paradox of prescribing the symptom—an action that is inapplicable for the stated reasons—our principle of double transparency in the relationship between the client and the referring social service excludes resorting to any paradox. Part of our job is to keep the judge precisely informed about anything that occurs in our relationship with the clients; this goal, which is fundamental to our task, prevents the use of any measures having a provocative aim. And paradoxical prescription, paradoxical forecast, and even mere reframing each have a provocative function.

They are methods for deconstructing the significant elements of family dynamics and reconstructing them in a different way. The therapist strives to give the family dynamics a plausible interpretation that the members do not expect and that can therefore introduce new input into the system.

However, the therapist who resorts to this method will in no way address the problem of the "truth" of what she asserts. By taking an epistemological approach that is rigorously constructivist, she is suggesting a reading of the familial events that would revolutionize the useless explanation that the family has previously come up with.

The constructivist approach is prohibited for any expert called upon to present an opinion to the court. Indeed, when asking the expert what she feels may have triggered the maltreatment in the family, the court is following a typically positivist line of thinking.

When our team had to choose between constructivist relativism and scientifically outmoded positivism, we opted for a co-constructivist approach (Speed, 1984). In so choosing, one is quite aware that the observer influences both the object observed and his own observation. This consciousness is therefore immune to the positivist illusion that reality can be photographed as is. As we pointed out in Chapter IV, we renounced a priori any goal of offering the judge a description of how the family "really" functions, independently of ourselves; our aim is to report on how the family reacts to our intervention.

On the other hand, we do not evade the court-mandated assignment to bring out, through our intervention, the distinctive features that organize the family's internal relationships—that is, its game—in such a way as to generate abuse. Now this game, as an inevitable modality of the interactive organization of any "group-with-a-history," exists independently of the therapist's intervention. As a result, it can be tracked down, albeit with a certain degree of approximation, and reconstructed in a nonarbitrary manner.

In the book that we have often quoted, Selvini Palazzoli and her collaborators (1989) describe the evolution of their theory and technique. Abandoning the use of paradox, they adopted a co-constructivist perspective and followed a multidimensional line of thinking that transcends mere systemic purism. In a less meditated and more intuitive way, our own team was impelled by contextual circumstances to immediately shelve the paradoxical method; instead, we pinned our hope and confidence on grasping the intricate complexity underlying the phenomenon of abuse.

Prescriptions at the Early Sessions

In mandated treatment, it is impossible not only to resort to paradoxical techniques, but, unfortunately, to make use of prescriptions. Traditionally, prescription is viewed as the instrument par excellence of family therapy, which is classified among the prescriptive therapies. But in a mandated context, the client's unwillingness to seek help completely voids the therapist's power to prescribe. If, indeed, coercion can actually make the client report to our Center, it cannot force her to obey the suggestions of our team. Even if not openly clashing with the therapist's right to assign tasks (a right upheld by the judge's order), the client has a thousand ways of sabotaging it. Far more often than in spontaneous therapy, a person who is forced into treatment can blame others for making it impossible to follow a therapeutic prescription. A client can lie, she can pretend she went through with it, she can implement it in such a way as to undermine or destroy its effectiveness, etc. Obviously, the therapeutic team has no possibility of countering these efforts by breaking off the treatment—a step that might be considered in a voluntary context! Mandated therapy has to renounce any prescriptive character, at least in an initial phase, when it has still to inspire an authentic collaboration in the clients.

Nevertheless, it often happens that our team resorts to prescriptions at the earliest meetings, but we have no illusions that the clients will obey. Our goal is actually to focus their attention on several problem areas whose very existence they keep denying.

One example is the Puglisi-Bisceglie case that we have already described on pp. 52–55. With Christmas just around the corner, the parents kept asking us if they could have their children home for the holidays. Our team suspected that the parents desired this visit chiefly in order to confuse their relatives by making it seem that the children were actually attending "boarding school" at the free choice of the parents. Naturally, when informed of the team's impression, the parents strenuously denied such motives. On the other hand, neither the district social worker nor the officials of the institution housing the children saw any contraindications to having the children visit their parents from morning to evening on Christmas Day. Turning down this request would have exacerbated the reactivity of the parents, who had already once practically abducted the youngest son from the residential center.

Consequently, the therapeutic team stated that they had informed the judge that they were favorable to the idea of the visit, provided the spouses made an effort to show the children that they were establishing a nuclear family, which they had never developed. They would have to be willing to spend Christmas as a nuclear family, inviting no other kin and no friends. The parents agreed: the father enthusiastically; the mother, as was obvious, only for expedience. What actually happened? Several days before Christmas, Mrs. Bisceglie provocatively told Mr. Puglisi that if her mother invited her to Puglia for the holidays, she, Mrs. Bisceglie, would leave him and the children in Milan and head south. As we can guess, Mr. Puglisi hit the roof; he beat his wife once again, and they separated for the nth time. Naturally, "for the sake of the children," the two reconciled on Christmas Day; however, each parent took one child and went to visit her or her own relatives. Their conduct, discussed in the first session after Christmas, enabled the team to gather data in order to show the two parents that *each of them*, and not only Mrs. Bisceglie, put his or her respective family of origin above any new nuclear family.

Thus, a first useful effect of a prescription can be to disclose—by the refusal to carry it out—the presence of problem areas that are stubbornly denied. Indeed, once the clients have accepted the prescription, they cannot maintain that they have failed to comply for lack of desire (that is, ignoring the therapist's authority); rather, they have to acknowledge the existence of a difficulty in following the prescription.

There is one domain that can be highly revealing about these "impossible" structural prescriptions[2] — that is, the kind that clearly tend to define the boundaries of the family. This domain is that of reconstituted families. A high percentage of our clients are unmarried parents who live together after one of them has been through a failed marriage. Frequently, the abuse in such cases is triggered by a climate of veiled and unspoken resentment: One partner (usually, but not always, the woman), wishes to legalize the relationship, while the other one keeps citing complex bureaucratic obstacles that are mere pretexts.

A situation that was extreme even within our highly dramatic caseload was that of the family of Angela and Calogero, who had been referred to our Center because of the very serious abuse of their daughter, Carmelina. The school physician had found whip marks all over the back of the seven-year-old girl. Carmelina was psychotic, incontinent, and almost unable to speak. It was very hard to determine which of the parents had beaten her; both of them obstinately denied doing it, and Calogero repeatedly threatened the school principal, saying he would get even with her for notifying the authorities.

Carmelina's parents had first met after Calogero's wife, Rosa, had walked out on him, taking along their six-year-old son, Vincenzo. Rosa was carrying the baby of another man, who had mortally insulted poor Calogero, accusing him of being impotent and homosexual. It was during that time, when he

2. In family therapy, the structural school can be traced back chiefly to the works of Minuchin, one of the pioneers of the family therapy movement. His works have greatly influenced Italian therapists, especially Maurizio Andolfi and his colleagues in Rome.

had been foaming with rage, that Calogero had met Angela. Their meeting turned out to be providential for him because Angela was two months pregnant. She had been deserted by a soldier, who had "classically" fled when informed of her pregnancy. Thus, in court, at the first separation hearing, Calogero had been able to oppose Rosa's "big belly" with his financée's almost equally prominent belly; in this way, he could erase any shame.

Calogero had obviously promised Angela that he would both marry her and acknowledge her baby, a girl named Maria. Later on, however, he told Angela that he would go through with the acknowledgment and the marriage once he divorced his first wife. Thus, Maria remained illegitimate despite the fantastic theories that Calogera concocted to persuade himself, Angela, and their relatives that the little girl was sort of his natural daughter because during the first three months, "the seeds mix. . . . "

One year later, Carmelina was born, and then three more children followed in rapid succession. At this point, Angela's parents, who lived in the country, were given permanent custody of Maria. This seemed like a balancing of accounts, for Calogero had lost his own son, Vincenzo, while Angela now gave up her own daughter.

It soon became increasingly obvious that poor Angela was sinking into a deeper and deeper depression as she slowly grew more aware that Calogero was simply using her. Time passed, but she did not become his wife, she was nothing but the girl whom he flaunted at Rosa, the betrayer: Calogero was using Angela chiefly to rehabilitate his manliness in the eyes of all his kinfolk. His mother and his sisters missed no opportunity to remind Angela that she was not married and that she didn't deserve it anyway, because she had had a daughter by another man. Furthermore, they constantly disqualified her as a housekeeper and, above all, as a mother.

Needless to say, Calogero, who was big on talk and short

on action, never dared to defend Angela against his own intimidating mother. He would have been delighted to hand the children over to their grandmother if only she had really wanted them. She kept stirring up his hopes, but she never took any concrete steps in this direction. Above all, she kept saying that she could work miracles with Carmelina, who was living proof of Angela's failure as a mother: The girl spoke badly, did not know how to clean herself, never paid attention. . . . Was it any wonder that wretched Angela went so far as to wish her daughter dead and came very close to killing her?

Despite this reconstruction, which was sufficiently clear and complete for the therapeutic team, the treatment was on the verge of failure because both parents obstinately denied that Angela had whipped the girl. The couple stopped showing up for sessions, and for two years we thought we had lost them altogether. Carmelina, whose placement with a foster family did not work out, was transferred to a specialized institution, the location of which was kept secret from her parents. The couple, by no longer attending the diagnostic sessions at our Center, had, to all intents and purposes, given up seeing their daughter. But then one day, Calogero, whose mother kept rekindling his vacillating sense of honor, decided to consult a lawyer in order to assert his right to know Carmelina's whereabouts and to visit her. His attorney persuaded him to petition the judge to resume the evaluatory meetings. When the two parents came back to us, they were more defensive than ever. Indeed, they stubbornly denied the existence of any problem before the therapist managed even to speak a single word. After a few sessions, Calogero, exasperated by the team's continuous efforts to shed light on the family's problems, threatened to bring his own lawyer to the next meeting. Contrary to his expectations, the team took him seriously and showed great relief at his supposed intimidation: They contacted his attorney and set up a joint meeting.

Not only did the intelligent lawyer do an excellent job of assuming the beneficial role of intermediary, but his presence at the session was infinitely useful, because it allowed the therapist to express all his own doubts about Calogero's position on remarrying. Why had he not obtained his divorce after seven years of legal separation? Why did he still refuse to acknowledge Maria? Why did he not bring Vincenzo home for visits? The lawyer, who at first did not even know of the existence of Calogero's estranged wife or of Vincenzo and Maria, promised to inform himself, while Calogero shrank visibly and Angela seemed about to levitate from her chair.

From that session on, the team literally showered poor Calogero with prescriptions. He was to bring Vincenzo home with him on a Sunday, since, as our Center ascertained, such visits were not only permitted, but actually stipulated by the separation agreement! He also had to show up for sessions with little Maria: Given his intention of making her his daughter as soon as possible, she would have to get accustomed to being with the family. Above all, he and Angela had to discuss his reasons for not marrying her, since the divorce decree—requested by Rosa and not by him—had been filed two years earlier.

As we have said, the team had no illusions that these restructuring prescriptions would be more than minimally carried out. However, his failure to implement them would unequivocally show the reluctant Calogero that problems—and what problems!—did indeed exist.

Revealing the Game

From what has been said, it is clear that the chief therapeutic tool, the one from which we anticipate so much, consists of revealing the game. In fact, from the start of our activity, and for the reasons illustrated above, we had to do without two tactics for inducing change: paradox (as well as any other provocative form of reformulating or reframing) and prescriptions. Our armory of interventions thus left us, in substance, the possibility of exposing the game.

Until some time ago we profoundly distrusted other pedagogical and rehabilitative methods, such as were frequently used, for example, by the team of Odette Masson, whom we have repeatedly quoted. Those methods struck us as mere palliatives in contrast with our fundamental supposition that a family was perfectly capable of reorganizing itself on its own once it was freed of pathogenic ties. Yet our relentlessly optimistic outlook was subsequently modified.

At this point, we ought to specify what we mean by "revealing the game." There is no need to cite an example: All the descriptions of family games, as presented in Chapter V, could serve as instances of exposure. Naturally, the verbalization must be steered in such a way that the reconstruction is easily grasped by the patients, just as it must occur in the appropriate emotional atmosphere.

Revealing a game is a radically different approach from a psychoanalytic interpretation. Psychoanalysis offers insight into a transferential relationship between analysand and analyst, while the exposure of a game takes place during a family session, at which every member of the group is confronted with a revelation about the covert aims of his or her own strategies, as well as those of other members. In our opinion, this difference is the basis of the potential efficacy of exposure in a mandated context. Obviously, in coercive treatment, nothing can be usefully interpreted or explained to a lone client. In fact, if an unrequested intervention is made, the lone client who has asked for nothing will respond by refusing, disqualifying, minimizing, and/or closing himself off. In a family session, this person can, of course, exhibit the same behavior—but he will have to deal with the fact that family members, together with him, have heard the therapist's statements about his strategies, and it is not certain that the others will react with the same denials! Indeed, when it comes to revealing the family game, each member will tend to reject any disagreeable aspect that concerns him- or herself, but he or she can enthusiastically embrace any unpleasant facts that are revealed about other members—if only to exculpate or justify him- or herself. In this way, each member supplies the therapist with material corroborating various facets of his or her own exposure. This enables the therapist to reframe, retouch, perfect, and reinforce the exposure, thereby making the reconstruction of the game more convincing.

Furthermore, each family member, whether immediately at the session or subsequently at home, will be inspired to assume a behavior that belies the therapist's statements. At best, the mutual influence of such changes, however reactive they may be, will lead to a more or less substantial modification of the game.

Obviously, a complex game, like the one that sustains maltreatment, is not brought to light all at once. Often, the exposure that concludes the diagnostic phase is limited to a very general outline of the strategies employed by individual members of the family. However hard the team may try to pinpoint the details, the reconstruction can still be too general to effect a radical change.

Likewise, when a game is exposed, the aspect that is brought out may be the most blatant one—for instance, the way the spouses play a significant relative against each other. But this level of the game may have been worn down over the years, and if the spouses each decide to stop involving the old ally, their renunciation will no longer be determining. Indeed, not infrequently, old coalitions are restructured when the children get embroiled.

We had the case of a very young couple, whose three children were chronically neglected, one being episodically abused by the father during his fights with his wife. The game brought to light by the team during the third session showed—a bit stereotypically—that the war between the young spouses could be traced back to their unresolved ties with their respective parents. After this intervention, the husband (the only son amid four sisters) had finally given up on an old project, which he had obstinately tackled over his wife's furious objections. He had planned to bring his mother from the south for medical treatment, thereby getting her away from her tyrannical husband, with whom he had always battled, regularly losing.

At the same time, his young wife had unexpectedly decided to spend their welfare money on a washing machine. This meant giving up her two weekly visits to her mother's house (to bring, and then call for, her laundry); during these visits, she had let off steam about the wrongs inflicted on her by her husband. In this way, the young woman had imagined that she was gaining, if not the affection, then at least the compassion of her mother, who was completely absorbed in her four sons.

These changes struck the therapeutic team as relevant for their prognosis, partly because the husband got a regular job—his first after 12 years of marriage—and the wife emerged from years of apathy, in which she had shown no interest in either their home or their children. On the other hand, while abandoning old alliances, the two spouses did not commit themselves to building a solid couplehood. Their only expression of cohesiveness was joint hostility toward the common enemy represented by institutions: the school that had reported them, the court of law, the social agencies. Both husband and wife simply reinforced their nascent favoring of their offspring: Each parent openly selected one of the two older children as a vicarious spouse and used that child more and more in a coalition against the other spouse. Once the evaluative phase was terminated, that was the next level of the game that had to be revealed and addressed during the actual therapy.

A Determining Intervention: Defining the Format of the Therapy

While our therapeutic armory may be extremely limited in regard to mandated treatments, the exposure of the game is not our only weapon; we can also decide who is to participate in the sessions. Contrary to what one might think, this is an extremely effective intervention. As a result, it is quite delicate, requiring our team to make anything but automatic choices.

When we started out, our summons followed the practice developed by Selvini Palazzoli. Aside from strictly defined exceptions, her team invites the nuclear family and any significant relative(s) to the first session, then only the parents and the children to a few—normally two—subsequent sessions, and finally only the parents. Very soon, however, it became obvious that our adherence to this model had no raison d'être in our context. The therapies at Selvini's center are meant for a gravely symptomatic child or, more often, adolescent, for whose cure the two parents—implicitly or explicitly—are made to share responsibility. In this way, the parents become their child's therapists to the extent that they modify their own couplehood and/or interrupt their child's involvement in their relationship.

But in our case work, the opposite is true. We deal not with a child's pathology, but with a symptom, her abuse, presented by one or both parents. The abuse is not infrequently accompanied by other psychiatric symptoms, such as alcoholism, drug addiction, depressions, and/or psychoses, in either the abusive parent, the spouse, or both. Finally, in many cases, the specific pathology marks the relationship of the couple, who live in open conflict, have violent and explosive fights, yet are incapable of going through with a real separation—not just in legal terms.

In all these instances, our choice of working with both parents would not mean that we are allying ourselves with people who want to help a child, that we are trying to get them to admit that they have unconsciously triggered his pathology by involving him in their marital troubles. Quite the contrary. In our case such a choice would bluntly confirm what the family already knows—namely, that the actual patients, the ones who are really ill, are the parents who, deeply embroiled in their dreadful conflict, are abusive, mentally frail, socially deviant, etc.

What we need, case by case, are extremely diversified therapeutic strategies, that prevent, as far as possible, erroneous invitations from crystallizing an already universally shared definition of who the real patients are. To determine these strategies, we follow this fundamental criterion: We always consider all three generations of the family and, depending on the case, we select the generational level on which we feel it would be most useful to work.

Let us investigate a few examples of the various alternatives. In so doing, we must bear in mind that in the course of a treatment, it may prove advisable to switch from one format to another, for instance extended families, nuclear family, couple, then back to nuclear family, and so forth.

Alternating Sessions with the Two Extended Families

A well-known basic therapeutic goal is to get the parental couple away from relatives' interference. Yet the family therapy centers keep observing that the families applying for help are usually in the category of "enmeshed" families (Minuchin, 1974); for them, the therapists readily determine a need to mark the boundaries that distinguish them from extended families. Often, this means a clan whose members jointly run an industrial or commercial business, live in the same patriarchal home or in contiguous apartments, spend their vacations together, gather for celebrations, telephone one another a lot, and so forth.

In contrast, most of the families coming to the district social services like our Center can be classified as so-called "disengaged" families (Minuchin, 1974), in which the processes of disintegration have resulted in extremely sporadic contacts among the various members of the original families. Often, the abusive or neglectful parents have grown up in institutions or have geographically distant, sometimes separated parents, with whom they rarely communicate. Occasionally, they complain about the esteem or privileged treatment that a sibling receives from their parents while they themselves are never consulted.

Our in-depth work with this second group of families has induced us to set aside Minuchin's distinctions between enmeshed and disengaged families; in our opinion, his distinction is too descriptive to allow for differentiated clinical choices. For instance, we have frequently noticed that certain unsatisfactory bonds are difficult to resolve; for this reason, an extreme paucity of contact with the extended families is very often accompanied by an agonizing regret, a veiled and unexpressed resentment—in short, an infinitely greater emotional intensity than either of the spouses invests in the conjugal bond.

Thus, in the case of an apparently disengaged family, we must do our best to bring out the invisible clan ties that perniciously interfere with the formation of the conjugal couple.

With this clear objective in mind, we abandoned the standard practice of inviting one or more members of the extended family to the opening session. In such unusual and complex circumstances as those of mandated evaluation, we find it more advisable to summon the nuclear family, but to talk to the parents first. We tell them about the goals and procedures of our work, and we use the presence of their children to give them—and, indirectly, everyone—further elements for clarifying the overall context.

First of all, the parents are told that the therapist's objective is to help them by discovering if there is a possibility of bringing the children back home. It is only after the work of reassuring the family has gotten underway that we find it useful to summon the extended families.

During the years in which the context-explaining session included the presence of an important relative, we ascertained that the parents often acted far more aggressively toward the social workers and therapists. The reason was that they had to defend their parental image in front of the extended family, which often had secretly applied very severe criticism to them. In an evaluative context, the kinfolk go along with their relative's protest in order to prevent him from losing his children. As a result, the parents and the relatives virtually incite one another against the professionals. This unrelenting defense makes it almost impossible for us to use the presence of kinfolk for deepening our analysis of the relations within the families of origin. On the contrary, when the parents, arriving for the second session, feel less threatened because they more readily understand the potential helpfulness of the diagnostic context, they communicate less alarm even to their own relatives.

Therefore, at our first meeting, we suggest, if possible, two appointments, spaced not too far apart, with the respective family of each spouse.[3] Not infrequently, both spouses are astonished that the

3. We have encountered an intriguing analogy between our practice and the model of couple therapy suggested by Canevaro (1988). However, there are major differences between these two types of intervention; the most important distinction is that Canevaro excludes the spouse from his or her partner's family-of-origin session and tries to keep the contents of that session a secret from the other family.

therapists would want to know their relatives, especially when their own contacts with them are so sporadic. Quite often, they state that it would be impossible to convince their kinfolk to participate, or else they fiercely refuse to invite them. Yet at the same time, they are surprisingly willing to furnish a mother's or sister's phone number, while asserting that they never call one another. They know the number by heart or else have it written on a slip of paper that is scrupulously folded in a wallet. In a word, they seem torn between two emotions: They hope that our social worker, perhaps by alluding to the court, will manage to convince the reluctant relative to get involved, yet they fear that the "mess" they are in with the institutions will make them lose that bit of esteem that they still have in the eyes of their kinfolk. In other cases, they foresee that their own parents will only rebuke and criticize them, and will offer at most a perfunctory word of help or defense. Or else, they will be too ashamed to show the degradation of their own relatives: alcoholism, prostitution, etc.

The therapist is often too easily discouraged by this resistance; but if she can overcome it, the session with the members of the extended family usually turns out to be extremely informative. The strategy at this meeting consists of making all the participants aware of the following problem: The unresolved ties that one of the spouses keeps up with his family of origin may constitute a serious interference, both past and present, with the functioning of the nuclear family. The material emerging at this session can prove illuminating, especially for that person's spouse.

Let us examine the case of a man whom we shall call Augusto Valliani. At a very young age, he married Loredana, who was equally young and already the unmarried mother of a two-year-old boy. Loredana had been raised in an orphanage, and her infrequent contacts with her mother and the latter's successive live-in boyfriends had always been tumultuous. When she met Augusto, Loredana's son was with a foster mother, to whom she was deeply attached. After five years of marriage and the births of two daughters, Augusto could still not understand why Loredana insisted on leaving the boy with the foster mother—of whom he was acutely jealous—rather than having him live with them. Loredana claimed that her husband and her son would never get along; yet it was she who abused the child after yet another fight with her husband.

At the session to which Loredana's mother was summoned, the therapist succeeded in showing that the young woman's attachment to the foster mother was aimed at arousing the jealousy not so much of her husband as of her mother. And even though Loredana's marriage was on the rocks, she insistently pursued her strategy because her mother always seemed about to take the bait. Now, her mother had never attended any of the baptisms of her three grandchildren; nor had she ever been willing to take care of them even during Loredana's emergency hospitalization; and, finally, she claimed that she was deeply attached to her three dogs but did not love her grandchildren. Nonetheless, in an ambivalent and contradictory manner, she stated that if her grandson had to be farmed out to a stranger (the foster mother), he'd be better off with his grandmother, even though he wa so energetic and she was getting old.

Her tepid words were enough to rekindle Loredana's illusion that, 25 years after putting her in an orphanage, her mother would finally change and take care of her through the little boy. When Augusto at last understood this dramatic bond, which indissolubly made Loredana her mother's prisoner, he had a clear idea of the overall situation. That is, he could try behaving differently, rather than opposing the foster mother like a sulky child, or clashing with his stepson and feeling guilty for not being affectionate enough toward him, or acting childish and spiteful toward his wife. It was only by actively supporting Loredana that he could help her develop a different rapport with her mother, and with fewer expectations and therefore fewer frustrations.

At the same time, it was only her husband's understanding and solidarity that could induce Loredana to turn to him for affection rather than continue her sterile attempts to get affection from her mother.

After conducting a session like the one described above, we often fell into a trap, due to the significance of the game that one spouse was playing with her own family. This significance can lead us to overlook the partner's complementary game, which adapts to and intersects with the first game. In fact, if Augusto, at such a young age, chose to marry a girl with a child, but failed to meet her emotional needs in any way, we would have to investigate the reasons.

The next session included Augusto's younger sister, who shared her brother's role as black sheep of the family. This meeting helped the therapists by illustrating the maze of relationships in the preceding generation of the Vaillianis.

Their family life was dominated by the mother and Rolanda, the eldest girl, who formed a couple, in which neither the father nor the other three daughters had any say. Augusto, the second youngest child and the only son, maintained a silent solidarity with his father, prodding him to rebel against the mother's and Rolanda's domination. Disappointed by his father's passivity, Augusto grew all the more rebellious himself, ultimately becoming a good-for-nothing with little desire to work; he hung out with a bad element and had several run-ins with the law (driving without a license, thefts of mopeds, etc.). His marriage to Loredana, a rebellious girl with a child in tow, was one more way of provoking his family, in which Rolanda, who was married but childless, not only continued to rule the roost, but had gotten her husband accepted as a "real" son with "a good head on his shoulders" and capable of giving help and advice. No wonder then that Augusto was willing to stay involved in his family of origin, since his union with Loredana, being a marriage of revenge, had gotten off to a bad start.

At this session, Loredana, who was strong-willed and impulsive, came to realize that her fights with her mother-in-law and her furious arguments with her know-it-all sister-in-law were precisely what Augusto wanted of her: that is, an ulterior attack on the two matriarchs. At the same time, however, Loredana understood that her husband would never be grateful to her for this attack, given his secret and unavowed desire to obtain respect, and not pity, from his weak father as well as, just once in his life, a bit of the frequent praise that his mother bestowed on her pet son-in-law. But with a shaky marriage, an illegitimate son put out to a foster mother, and a frustrated wife who took her anger out on her boy, poor Augusto had little chance of achieving these goals.

When There Is Only One Extended Family: The Cross Coalition

In a few particularly insidious cases, the therapist, upon grasping the obvious game that one spouse is playing with his family of origin, vainly tries to understand the game that the other spouse is playing with her own family of origin. No matter how thoroughly the therapist may investigate, there are situations in which the members of one of the two extended families have all died or else are living so far away as to have virtually no relations with the nuclear family.

In such cases, if we are dealing with serious abuse or even a profound disturbance of the family order, we have to consider the possibility that both spouses are involved in a particularly harmful and malignant game with the same extended family.

Typical, in this sense, was the tragic situation of the Pasqua family, which was reported to Juvenile Court by a hospital pediatrician, who had treated little Debora, 15 months old, for convulsive fits. During the infant's hospitalization, her mother had given her various pills of an extremely toxic nature. The woman, in an obvious state of confusion, had then told the pediatrician that she "seemed to remember" that at home she had tried to suffocate the baby with a pillow—an episode that appeared to have triggered the onset of the fits and a slight hemiparesis in the little girl. Her mother, Grazia, diagnosed as suffering from a postpartum psychosis, was an intelligent and cultured young woman, and Debora was her first child. Grazia's husband, Franco, slightly younger than she and less educated, had migrated to Milan from southern Italy: he worked nights in a factory. Grazia had a job as a secretary; at the end of each day, she would pick her daughter up at the day-care center and then have dinner at her parents' place rather than staying home alone. She and Franco had always been very close to her family. Thus, after the hospital report, the judge placed the baby with Grazia's mother, who gave up her own job in order to care for her.

We won't bother going into detail about the nature of the game played by the young woman and her parents, partly because it closely resembles other games that we have described. Grazia was an only daughter, favored by her father, with whom she had a relationship marked by constant fights and arguments. She suffered because of the breach between herself and her mother—a breach that widened as the daughter grew closer to her father. When Grazia learned she was pregnant, she was reluctant to have her baby; but her husband pressed her to go through with it. Grazia told her mother, who reacted with great indifference, leaving it up to her daughter to decide whether or not to have an abortion. When Debora was born, her grandfather simply fell in love with her and relegated his daughter to second place. However, his "betrayal" and Grazia's failure to win back her mother did not seem to adequately explain why Grazia viewed her daughter as a hated rival whom she had to eliminate. It was only by analyzing Franco's relationship with Grazia's parents that we could see how Debora's birth had created a "scorched earth" around Grazia.

Franco was a very young man, who had gained independence from his family at an early age. However, as is often the case, his going out on his own at 15 signaled his profound alienation at home, where he played second fiddle to his older brother. Franco was initially disliked by his in-laws because of his southern origin and his working-class background of his southern origin and his working-class background, but his gentle and engaging character soon managed to win them over.

If Grazia had felt even a meager urge to emancipate herself from her family by forming a relationship, her desire was soon squelched by her husband, who, instead of expressing irritation at their frequent contacts with his in-laws, actively sought them out, overshadowing Grazia more and more in their eyes.

Very soon, Grazia's parents started seeing her as a reactive and impatient girl, whom Franco was kind enough to put up with. Likewise, Grazia's recriminations about his working at night, which, incidentally, he chose to do, appeared entirely unjustified to her parents. Thus, when Franco talked her into having a baby, Grazia, although dubious, gave in, hoping that the child would bring them closer together. But she was disappointed, for Debora's presence did not induce Franco to spend more time at home: He was quite content to let his in-laws take care of his daughter, thereby solidifying their bond with him.

In getting himself "adopted" by Grazia's parents, Franco evidently had two goals: He wanted compensation for his own parents' lack of interest in him, and he hoped that his parents would grew closer to him. And indeed, his parents, especially after the birth of their granddaughter, began acting warmer toward him, letting him know that they disapproved of his being absorbed into his wife's family.

Thus, Grazia found herself with a husband who was still committed to his own parents, yet she failed to understand why he was so interested in her parents and so uninterested in her. Furthermore, while both the men in her life—her father and her husband—fell madly in love with little Debora, Grazia's

mother did not. In fact—until the report of attempted infanti-
cide—the grandmother continued to show her granddaughter
the same indifference that she had displayed when dealing with
the unusual preference that her husband had exhibited toward
Grazia.

Thus, during the first few months after Debora's birth,
Grazia was profoundly disappointed and depressed. She dimly
felt robbed of everything that was hers by right: her husband,
her daughter, her father, her mother. But how could she react
to these thefts if her rivals were the very people that she longed
for? How could she complain that her husband and Debora
were depriving her of her father and her husband? The only
thing that Grazia could—and did—openly protest was her
mother's lack of interest in her grandchild. However, Grazia
could not openly lament her mother's lack of interest in her,
Grazia, since she herself, with her father's complicity, had contributed to alienating her mother!

In the bewilderment of her psychosis (and, mind you, no
one in the family suggested that she seek treatment), her protest
against those multiple desertions found an outlet—aggression
against her daughter: Debora should have regained those people's affections for Grazia, but instead, she seemed to have
robbed her mother of their affections.

The Grandparents as Co-therapists

In the two cases described above—Loredana and Augusto; Franco
and Grazia—the reader probably guessed that after the sessions devoted to reconstructing the game between the couple and the extended families, we stopped summoning the kinfolk and began working solely with the nuclear family. By choosing to deal only with
the couple, the team is explicitly declaring the following goal: to
determine whether husband and wife are capable of resolving their
own ties to their extended families and thus developing a satisfying
conjugal relationship. It is only by establishing such a relationship—
or, vice versa, by going through with a real separation—that the

two partners can assume their own parental responsibilities without relapsing into abuse or neglect of their offspring.

If the reconstruction of the game is sufficiently detailed and shared, the exclusion of the grandparents and the complete focus on the nuclear family is the next logical step, neither offending nor displeasing anyone involved. Later on, we will more fully describe the various therapeutic formats that can be selected once the grandparents are dismissed.

For now, we would like to illustrate an alternative formula: the dismissal of the parents and the focus on the grandparents. This alternative is considered seriously if the parents themselves are unusually young and/or seriously disturbed (alcoholics, drug addicts, psychotics) and if the grandparents strike us as more capable of benefiting from therapy. The changes achieved in the grandparents will help to modify the symptoms in the parents — including their unfitness as parents. By way of an example, let us outline the evolution of the following case.

Alessandra, an unmarried mother diagnosed as suffering from a symbiotic psychosis, was totally incapable of caring for her nine-month-old daughter. The 20-year-old mother, who lived with her parents, was at daggers drawn with her own mother, who was frequently hospitalized for recurrent depressions. The conflicts between the two women about looking after the infant were so intense that the baby was inadequately cared for.

Alessandra, who came from a family of tradesmen, had entered and abandoned various therapeutic treatments, but had not begun a new one for several years. It was the Family Planning Service that notified the court about the present situation. A few years earlier, at the age of 17, Alessandra, accompanied by her mother, had come to this office in order to interrupt her first pregnancy. A few months later, pregnant for the second time, Alessandra had reappeared, uncertain about whether or not to have another abortion; she decided against it.

After little Alice was born, Alessandra repeatedly asked the caseworkers to take the child away because Alessandra's mother prevented her from looking after the baby as she wanted to.

At this point the first meeting at our Center took place; it came about when the court ordered the removal of little Alice from her mother and her maternal grandparents and asked the social service department to find a suitable place for her. However, the judge permitted the agency to put Alice in a facility that could also house Alessandra. The young mother agreed to leave her parents' home along with Alice; but at the institution, the residential workers observed that Alessandra grossly neglected her baby and was always on the phone with her mother, relentlessly complaining and attacking her.

Our first evaluatory session included Alice, Alessandra, and her parents. The latter, who had consulted an attorney in order to prevent the removal of their granddaughter, were extremely hostile to attending the meeting. They were also dead set against involving their recently married older son, since they were absolutely unwilling to trouble him with the family problems caused by Alessandra.

At this session, Alice was constantly passed from the arms of one woman to the arms of the other. The baby's father, who was awaiting trial for selling drugs, had been unable to acknowledge the child, while Alessandra kept declaring provocatively that she intended to marry him upon his release from prison.

It took two sessions—extremely blunt and "combative" on our part—to bring out, at least partially, a distressing family picture, which we will sketch below.

Alessandra's father, Luigi, the only son of a widowed mother, married Silvia, who had a bad relationship with her own mother, who had always preferred her elder son. Luigi expected Silvia, who had led a very unhappy home life, to devote herself to him exclusively. But the very opposite occurred: His wife spent most of her time telephoning her mother and reproaching her. Silvia, in turn, was disappointed by Luigi:

Instead of dedicating himself entirely to her in order to compensate for what she had failed to get from her own parents, he constantly focused on his mother, who was very old.

Amid the unconcealed discontent of both partners, the situation dragged on for several years after the birth of their first child. When his wife became pregnant again, Luigi was opposed to her having the baby. However, Silvia, who had been farmed out to a wet nurse as an infant, decided against abortion: She was explicitly competing with her mother, demonstrating to her that she would succeed in taking care of both children.

During that period, Silvia's father, whom she considered her only ally in her family of origin, retired from his business and, in the subsequent financial distribution, he allowed his wife to brazenly favor their son. Luigi, instead of defending Silvia, knuckled under to the arrangement rather than let her parents accuse him of having married her for money.

When Alessandra was born, Silvia suffered her first depressive episode; her mother flatly refused to look after the baby because she had her hands full with her son's children. Alessandra was therefore raised by her paternal grandmother.

Tragically, the next generation presented the same, albeit aggravated family constellation that had afflicted Silvia's family. Alessandra was being raised by a grandmother, who, because she resented her daughter-in-law for taking away her only son, instigated the little girl against her mother. Luigi made things worse, showing Alessandra all the discontent of a weak man tormented by a cold, demanding, and also depressive wife.

During adolescence, Alessandra more openly displayed her hostility to her mother, expecting her father to imitate her or at least back her up. But Luigi did the opposite: To maintain his peace and quiet, he harshly castigated his daughter and defended his wife. Alessandra, feeling isolated and furious, came to understand the treachery of the man whom she had thought her ally; she started dimly realizing that not only her mother, but also her father, had long preferred her sensible older brother. It was at this point that her psychosis took hold of her.

Now, the exasperating arguments with her mother, from whom she was unable to separate, the failure at school, and the abandonment of any psychotherapy were joined by Alessandra's flights from home, her sexual promiscuity, her choice of a partner certain to displease her parents, and her pregnancies.

Finally, Alessandra deluded herself into thinking that her boyfriend and the baby she had by him could make up for all the injustices that she had suffered. But now came the extreme betrayal: It began dawning on her that both her mother and her father loved Alice deeply, were taking the child away from her, and were willing to leave their own daughter to her wretched fate provided they did not lose their little granddaughter. This led to Alessandra's ambivalence toward Alice, her neglect, and the temptation to abandon her.

After bringing this dramatic situation to light, our team decided to suggest that the parents work together with the team in order to save Alessandra, partly by giving up their granddaughter. Alessandra was excused from coming to further sessions, and her parents struggled desperately under the extremely harsh constriction: If they wanted to save their daughter, they would have to completely renegotiate their own relationship, cut off their unresolved ties to their families of origin, and stop favoring their older son. The parents might be able to help cure their daughter by revolutionizing the very foundations of their own lives. Once they succeeded, Alessandra could gain her independence from them and take adequate care of Alice. Nevertheless, by going through with it, Alessandra's parents would lose any chance of starting from scratch, wiping out the past, annulling Alessandra, and replacing her with their granddaughter. On the other hand, if they refused to challenge themselves and alter their own lives, then there would be no hope for Alessandra. The court, aware of the serious risk that Alice might repeat her mother's fate, could then decide to remove the child definitively from her unfit mother and put her up for adoption. Luigi and Silvia, trapped between Scylla and Charybdis, chose therapy, which they had never accepted in the past, despite endless suggestions from specialists who had been consulted.

Two years later, Alessandra had made notable progress and was taking care of her daughter in an apartment entrusted to her by her parents. When Alessandra was at work, Alice, in accordance with the judge's order, stayed at a day-care center rather than with her grandmother.

This case is still a long way from being fully resolved, because Alice's father was recently let out of prison; this calls for an overall reassessment of the situation. Furthermore, Alessandra's parents, during two years of being genuinely involved in therapy, have shown the same motivations and/or resistance of any couple in spontaneous treatment. A caseworker has regularly kept tabs on Alessandra since her case was first reported to the court; and recently, Alessandra told the caseworker that she would like to consult a psychologist who could help her define her own relationship with Alice's father. The little girl, well looked after, sociable, and precocious in her psychomotor development, is monitored at the day-care center and through home visits by the caseworker.

Joint Sessions with Parents and Children

Freeing a child from participating in the parental game is a prime therapeutic goal whenever the child plays an active role in the game that triggers the abuse. We described several such games in Chapter V (pp. 107–114).

For some families, our top priority may be to halt the child's entanglement in the couple's conflict; we must therefore quickly try to disrupt the interactive circuit in which the mistreatment arises.

Nevertheless, we have decided to illustrate this objective only now because the child's involvement in the parental game is, obviously, never the first step in the dysfunctional evolution of a familial system. In fact, during the initial period of a couple's life, there may be no children, or the children may be too young to be cast in or volunteer for the role of confidant, defender, vicarious spouse, or what have you; as a result, it is normally the members of the family of origin who are then incited and/or offer to assume these roles.

At the same time, we may hypothesize that if a married couple has functioned for years by including a member of the extended family as the third party in a conflictual relationship, they will tend to keep reproducing this triangular configuration indefinitely. Thus, whenever the triangulated family loses either parent or both through death or old age, that loss is made good by whichever child seems most apt or inclined to perform the same function.

Like the preceding therapeutic goal of combating interference from kinfolk in the marital bond, the objective of terminating the child's involvement in the parents' relationship (a role that is damaging to them and especially to the child) can be pursued by means of various treatment formats.

The first format—the classical one of family therapy—involves joint sessions with parents and offspring. After clarifying the context with the caseworker and the family nucleus, we delve more deeply—if necessary, with selected representatives of the families of origin—into the relations between the nucleus and the two clans. It is only at this point that we move on to several sessions with parents and children. We will now describe the most typical of such sessions (examples of which were already given in Chapter V): Their aim is to disclose the child's active role in the parental-couple game.

Take little Claudio, who feels he has to defend his mother against his father's bullying: or take the boy of the same age who does his best to secretly get his father back to the house from which his ex-wife has thrown him out: Both children are victims of the wrong perspective. Each is actually convinced that by siding with the parent who seems victimized by the other parent's harassment, he will, if not succeed in guaranteeing the proper functioning of the family, at least manage to stave off the worst. And the child actively sacrifices himself to this goal. This is not the paradox of reframing the symptom of the so-called identified patient as an unconscious sacrifice. In fact, the child concretely jeopardizes his own relationship with a parent, by making him or her feel unjustly abandoned or attacked by him. The child risks this parent's disapproval or even reprisal in the form of abuse; he loses his serenity, his joyfulness, his childhood right to a protected life outside of adult arguments, his willingness to focus on himself, on his friends, on school.

In the sessions devoted to explaining the game, our goal is to help the child understand that his sacrifice, rather than achieving the intended results, actually does the opposite. It perpetuates the futile fight between his parents—a fight in which the presumed victim likewise inflicts blows that, although silent and concealed, are as murderous as the obvious ones inflicted by the supposed tormentor.

When the therapist is certain that the child has understood, she can dismiss him from the session together with his siblings. She explains that she and her colleagues will try for a while to take on the job of helping the parents to clarify their own relational difficulties and to find a way of getting out of them. This dismissal of the child has the thrust of an important intervention because it—usually—addresses minors who have already been removed from their parents and placed in an institution.

The unequivocal message is as follows: During the temporary removal of the children from home, the parents, aided by experts, must work to change themselves and their marital relationship, while the children remain spectators rather than acting as promoters or protagonists. Thus, we have at times been informed, in a subsequent session, that the children, including the little ones, had told their residential workers, with obvious emotion, that on that day "Papa and Mama were going to therapy." Several children had even explicitly voiced their hope that their parents would decide to change if they loved them!

It can certainly be upsetting to hear such a statement from a child who implicitly—or at times openly—accuses a parent of not loving her, because the parent continues to drink, take drugs, or beat his wife. Yet the ability to express himself in this way corresponds to a basic stage in the abused child's growth process, which has been seriously warped. In this stage, the child comes to realize that it is the parents' job to guarantee as far as possible the most suitable conditions for a serene family life—and not vice versa, as the child may have once confusedly but firmly believed.

The Intervention Applied to the Child after His or Her Dismissal from the Family Sessions

Naturally, in order to perform the task he has assumed in regard to the children, the therapist has to make sure that they are periodically kept abreast of how the treatment is developing. Sometimes, when parents visit them, the children are given an adequate opportunity to verify the situation directly. Or else they are sufficiently brought up to date by the news they receive from their foster parents, their residential workers, or their social workers.

That was what happened with Paolo, the fourth child in a family, who was much younger than the first three offspring—two girls and a boy. These older ones caused their parents a lot of trouble because of their drug addiction and their resultant deviant behavior (drug pushing, prostitution, theft) and incarcerations.

Prior to Paolo's removal at the age of seven, he had regularly been left at home and missed school, because his mother, an alcoholic, was still asleep, while his father and siblings claimed that it was her job, and not theirs, to drop him off at school. Furthermore, during subsequent visits to their home, the health-care worker had repeatedly found Paolo alone, running a high fever, amid incredible filth and disorder.

The diagnostic work with the family showed that the mother's chronic alcoholism was a sort of retaliation against her husband. After taking her out of an orphanage at a very young age and giving her several years of happiness, he had then made her play second fiddle to his parents and subsequently their three eldest children. Several dramatic sessions, attended first by the entire family and then only by the couple, were intensely devoted to reconstructing the family game—but to no avail. Neither parent would move from his or her entrenched position. The husband insisted that the family troubles were caused exclusively by the wife's alcoholism, which justified and explained the children's drug addiction; the wife meanwhile kept proclaiming that she had never made the least effort to go on the wagon or take care of the house because her husband had driven out the older children.

After obtaining our team's diagnosis that the spouses were beyond recovery, the Juvenile Court deprived them of custody of Paolo. The judge blamed the parents for refusing to follow the prescriptions and thereby modify their own behavior in order to guarantee their son's serene growth.

The caseworkers informed Paolo of the failure of his parents' therapy and the consequent steps taken by the judge. When other members of the family came to visit him, the residential workers helped the boy to understand the various problems: his mother's stubborn silence and persistent bitterness; the fatuous arrogance of his brothers and sisters, who were strengthened by their father's support; the irresponsibility of his father, who, ignoring Paolo during these visits, dozed off in an armchair or joked about with his oldest son. Yet it was the parents themselves who, after failing to get the judge's decision reversed and to meet the deadline for appealing, told the little boy, either singly or, sometimes, jointly: "Listen, Paolo, you may be the luckiest one of us all. Just look at our lives and the lives of your brothers and sisters! You'll be getting a different family." We believe that nothing could have more effectively helped the child to accept his new family than these tragic and deeply felt words.

At other times, if the children do not participate in the sessions, they may be unable to verify the parental situation adequately. It therefore becomes necessary for the therapist to invite the children to a joint session with their parents.

This was the case with two children, Laura, seven years old, and Igor, five years old, who were taken in at our Center because the boy had been abused by their father and both children had been seriously neglected by their mother.

The extremely young parents—he 24, she 22—lived in an apartment next door to the husband's family. His family had virtually adopted the young wife, who had lost both her own parents. At our Center, the two children were gradually helped to talk about and to elaborate on their dramatic experiences, which were linked to both parents. On the one hand, they knew that their father was a criminal, a professional thief, who had committed violent acts and been imprisoned several times; he also inflicted violence on his wife and his children. On the other hand, the children suffered from their mother's irresponsibility: She would leave them all alone in order to—literally and figuratively—follow her husband, who, adding insult to injury, cheated on her with other women.

Working with the couple turned out to be unexpectedly beneficial because they were highly intelligent and also deeply devoted to the treatment. The young woman in particular saw the couple's sessions as helping to get her husband to commit himself to her and taking him away from her mother-in-law, who, openly distrustful of institutions, was instigating her son to remove the children from our Center and bring them home.

As far as his wife was concerned, the young man's adherence to the rules of the context and his devotion to the treatment demonstrated his loyalty to her and his cautious escape from his mother's aegis.

During eight months of treatment, the wife was gradually able to express how satisfied she was that her husband seemed to "have his head screwed on right": He had found a regular job and was supporting her, he no longer went out at night without her, he had stopped using cocaine, and he had emotionally distanced himself from his domineering parents.

At the same time, the husband reported that his wife's attitude toward him had thoroughly changed: She was capable of self-criticism for the first time, she had stopped treating him like a missionary who has to convert an infidel, and she had become very attentive to the household and to their daughter's schooling.

Both parents were extremely punctual and solicitous when visiting their children at the Center and when carrying out all the measures suggested by the residential workers. Thus, together with the social service, we asked the judge to allow the children to visit their parents on weekends during a trial period. However, the residential workers noticed that, upon being informed that the court was to make a ruling that might return the children to their parents, the children took a clear turn for the worse. Igor was again plagued by recurring nightmares and resumed his aggressive behavior toward his companions, while Laura's school work immediately dropped off, and she had marked difficulties in eating. Both children anxiously looked forward to visits by their parents, whom they joyfully welcomed. But after such visits, the children would tell the residential workers about traumatic experiences they had had at home.

It appeared obvious that the prospect of weekends at home—an idea to which the children responded with joyful excitement—also aroused their fear. Since the children had not witnessed the process in which their parents had decided to re-establish the marital bond, they were afraid of reliving the traumas that they had previously experienced. We therefore decided to invite the children to a meeting with their parents in order to retrace with them the road taken by the couple.

Both children seemed to have trouble following what the therapist told them, despite the explanations that the parents, with his help, lavished on them. Distracted by the toys that were present in the room, the children replied in monosyllables; their behavior signaled that these matters did not concern them and that they would rather the adults discussed them among themselves. The therapist even asked the parents to stay behind the one-way mirror for a while (the children were already acquainted with it since they had sat behind it themselves, observing stretches of early sessions when they were disruptive or wanted to play). In this way, the children, although aware that their parents were watching them, grew a bit livelier, agreeing to talk to the therapist—somewhat formally, to be sure—about their fears of going home.

And yet, although the session appeared disappointing, it left a deep impact on the children, who made precise reports about it to the residential workers; very soon, the children seemed to have lost their earlier fears. Once the judge gave his consent, the weekend trial visits began, and there were no significant hitches. The children proved extremely unselfconscious in describing at the Center what had happened at home and in reporting in either setting on their experiences in the other. Several months later, during summer vacation, they returned home for a longer interval, four weeks. During their sojourn, the spouses met with the residential workers, even bringing up various problems that arose during the children's visit. Furthermore, the district social worker, who had the job of monitoring the visit, would come by periodically. Partly at her suggestion, the parents made several phone calls to the Center about small child-raising problems.

During the next school year, Laura and Igor returned home

permanently, while their parents continued their therapy and their psychoeducational meetings with the residential workers.

The Treatment of the Youngest Generation

The example of Laura and Igor introduces a further crucial implication of our treatment process: the need to reserve a few therapeutic moments specifically for the children if they do not participate in the family sessions. First of all, we feel that for Paolo, whose parents lost custody of him, as well as for Laura and Igor, we took the liberty of offering the reader a glimpse of our Residential Center, which is basically a therapeutic live-in center. During the period of treating a child, our residential workers and our educational psychologist are engaged in a series of daily interventions that go way beyond mere protection and support (however indispensable) in regard to the trauma of abuse and the child's consequent separation from his parents.

This encompassing therapeutic environment is carried over into the foster family if, as we have said, a positive prognosis requires a long treatment for the parents and therefore an extended removal of the minors from their home.

Aside from these two types of therapeutic help, a small—indeed very small—number of the children we deal with benefit from individual therapy. According to need, this individual therapy may begin while the child is staying at the Center or at an institution or after she returns to her parents. Obviously, this necessitates collaboration between the two types of therapy, with frequent meetings for scheduling and monitoring.

However, these specific cases are few and far between. More often, our team has found it useful to act on therapeutic insights in order to meet the needs of children who are excluded from sessions reserved for the adults in a family. This approach becomes even more urgent if treating the parents proves useless. In Paolo's case, our Center resolved to continue helping him through this dramatic situation; we extended his already lengthy stay during the custody proceedings when his parents tried to keep him. Upon losing custody, as we have said, they decided not to appeal the verdict. Paolo then remained with us until his adoption, so that, all told, he spent more than two years at our Center!

In other cases, however, we cannot count on analogous help for a minor when the court declares his parents to be unfit. At times, we feel that children are horribly "defenseless"–especially if adolescents are put up at boarding schools or institutions that are not equipped to guarantee them adequate help when they lose their families.

An emblematic case was that of a family that we shall call Loverso; it was made up of two parents and seven children– six daughters and one son–between the ages of 23 and 14. The three youngest children, who were repeatedly abused by their father, were removed by the authorities; two older daughters, who had left home for the same reasons, had managed to obtain the intervention of the social service even though they were over 18. While it was never proved, the father was suspected of having raped one of these two girls as "punishment" for her rebellious behavior.

The work with the family very quickly came to grief. We have never seen a married couple so inflexible and so hardened in mutual hatred. The husband, illiterate but possessed of a sharp and ruthless intelligence, was almost a caricature of a "padre-padrone," an excruciatingly despotic father. His wife, whose character dovetailed with his, was as stolid, stubborn, and obtuse as a beast of burden that refuses to budge no matter how harshly it is whipped. The six girls, all of them beautiful and intelligent, were consumed with hatred for their father, powerfully goaded as they were by the spectacle of their mother's passivity. The more she endured her husband's tyranny, the more she inspired the daughters' rebellion, which in turn provoked their father's rebukes and blows. On the other hand, the girls' feelings of pity for their mother were mixed with a profound disrespect for this apathetic woman, who was so lethargic even with them. Tragically, while they hated their father, they reluctantly admired his strength and intelligence and they yearned for even his slightest gesture of benevolence.

This tangle of emotions obviously made it impossible for the girls to achieve any psychological detachment from their parents. Two of the daughters remained physically at home. One girl endured her mother's furious outbursts against her husband, while the other girl was uselessly intent on pleasing this man, who deeply resented the two older girls for insulting him by leaving home. Now, physically these two daughters lived elsewhere; but despite the great importance they claimed they attached to their emancipation, they were unable to enjoy it: They were far too envious of the presumed emotional privileges of the sisters who remained at home. Two other daughters had been placed in a boarding school by the social service. One of these girls concentrated on building up a nest egg, hoping that this money would induce her father to take her back; the other girl dreamed of making her parents jealous by getting adopted by her fiancé's family.

This chaos of feelings left absolutely no space for sibling solidarity, mutual support, or consolation for the sister in greatest trouble. Their only emotions were envy, spite, and jealousy, and they would get trapped in dreadful imbroglios, or else two of the girls would form ever-changing coalitions against a third.

In this labyrinth, the brother, who, although the youngest child, was expected to be the "prince" of the house, went completely unnoticed. Perhaps less gifted than his sisters, and certainly ignored, he was unable to speak; blushing and weeping, he was more depressed and oppressed than any of the others. Deprived of a valid bond with his mother, the boy was crushed by his father's scorn. His sisters looked after him—not out of genuine interest, but more to compete with one another or to show their mother "how to do it."

Although we gave up all hope of changing the parents, we

did not wish to dismiss the children, who, in a very brief time, had shown profound interest in the family sessions. Early on, we tried to exclude at least the two daughters who had (seemingly) chosen to break off forever with their parents; but these two girls complained that our meetings were the only opportunities for all seven siblings to get together, chat, show one another the clothes they had bought, and talk about their future plans. We experienced a poignant moment when we read aloud our detailed negative prognosis about the family, in the presence of two caseworkers who were in charge of keeping up with the minors. After reading the long report, we handed out copies not only to the parents but also to each child; the text confirmed the collapse of the family, each member of which was now living on his or her own. But now the minor son had a wonderful idea: Every sister was to sign her name above the therapist's signature. In this way, each child, faced with mute and impassive parents, would endorse the document describing their agonizing family situation and the inexorable dispersion of what *could have been* a family.

Our work with the seven children was anything but fruitless. Its goal was to make them realize that they shared the same dramatic fate, even if they were struggling among themselves towards opposite solutions. We had agreed to stick with the boy until the social agency could locate foster parents willing to look after him until he came of age. We also managed to arouse noncompetitive feelings in at least several subgroups among the daughters, so that two of them eventually started rooming together. One of the girls also began individual psychotherapy, showing her sisters that it was possible to ask for help on one's own. Another girl notably improved her ability to establish positive relationships, both with her caseworker and at her boarding school.

The sisters were committed to visiting their brother regularly in his foster home; at the same time, they realized that they mustn't invade his new space. Those were further satisfying results.

The case of the Loverso family illustrates a procedure for treating the younger generation when we fail to make any headway with the parents. A chance to involve the offspring in the therapy may offer itself in other cases—for instance, when the couple's marital situation continually alters, and the children have to adjust to sharp and sudden changes as their parents separate, reconcile, break up again, and form new bonds. For some of these families, the therapist's office appears to provide the only place for rest, reflection, and dialogue, in which the participants manage to communicate their plans, mental states, and decisions.

We were confronted with the situation of the three Laurieto girls, who had been taken from their separated parents, broken up, and placed in institutions. The separation of the spouses had been triggered by the wife, who was sick of the constant fights with her alcoholic husband, the abuse he inflicted on her and on their two older daughters, and his chronic unemployment. The husband, who also had been on bad terms with his family of origin for years, was depressed and lonesome. He had never resigned himself to the couple's breakup, which had dashed any hopes he had of receiving even the appearance of affection, or at least companionship, from his wife and his daughters. Moreover, he took his wife's leaving him as an affront to his honor and prestige; his blood boiled at the mere thought that she might form a relationship with another man.

Thus, for Mrs. Laurieto, life after the separation proved as stressful as before: Her husband refused to leave their home, even though it had been awarded to her by the court, he harassed her at work in every possible way, he threatened her with a knife and a gun, and he beat her up several times.

Naturally, the wife acted in such a way as to keep alive in him the rather tenuous hope that, if "he turned over a new leaf," she would come back. When he was out, she would periodically visit the apartment to straighten it up for him and fix his supper; she would also agree to meet him in bars to discuss their relationship. Mrs. Laurieto never followed the advice of the social workers, who had been so helpful in getting her through her separation from her husband. They suggested that she take firm and decisive steps to cut all ties with her ex-husband, even use legal means to assert her rights. To make matters worse, whenever she had economic problems, she would ask her ex-husband for money, thereby feeding his illusion that she might once again become dependent on him. (Neither of them supported their daughters, who received welfare instead.)

Because of her immature and irresponsible behavior, Mrs. Laurieto was judged temporarily unfit to take care of her daughters, who were therefore placed in a boarding school, at the mercy of their mother's rare visits and their father's raids. Contrary to rules, he would show up every so often to take away the youngest child, Giada, and use the ten-year-old as bait to entice his wife to come to him. And she regularly fell for his maneuver. As for the two older girls, their father would threaten and insult them during his raids because, to his mind, they were siding with their mother. The three girls were thus forced to change schools three times, because the officials could not endure his drunken and violent intrusions: He would assault and bully them, then tearfully beg forgiveness the next day, thereby inducing these unfortunates not to report him to the police.

The early phases of treatment for this family were, as one can easily guess, extremely laborious. We will merely say that our least problem was to prevent Mr. Laurieto from waiting outside for his ex-wife after our sessions and beating her senseless. Nevertheless, within six months we managed to move from large sessions—involving the former nuclear family plus Mrs. Laurieto's father and mother, who played an important role in the situation—to several smaller meetings with only parents and children, and finally individual meetings with Mrs. or Mr. Laurieto. It was a titanic effort getting him to put up with separate appointments, since the joint sessions had offered him a chance to see his ex-wife. Yet to our surprise, it was she rather than he who then failed to keep the individual appointments: She would show up several hours too late or else stand us up without prior notice, while her ex-husband was a model of punctuality.

The following year, the situation gradually improved. Little by little, Mr. Laurieto stopped harassing his wife, and she stopped deluding him and letting him follow her. She began working more regularly, she organized herself to look for an apartment, and she no longer embroiled her eldest daughter in her own inconclusive romances—an involvement that exposed the girl to her father's angry outbursts and reprisals. Mr. Laurieto likewise began working with more continuity, he stopped invading his daughters' boarding school, and he finally agreed to regulated visitation rights, alternating with his wife in an arrangement that was sufficiently respected by both of them. Nevertheless, Mr. Laurieto could not overcome his depression or his alcoholism; yet he refused to see the district psychiatrist in a serious way or to join Alcoholics Anonymous.

In his profound and desperate solitude, his privileged relationship with little Giada, whom he had initially exploited as bait for his ex-wife, grew deeper, becoming his sole emotional resource. For the Easter holidays, both his ex-wife and the girl's boarding school, ignoring their agreement with the social service, gave in to Mr. Laurieto's special request: He wanted Giada to stay with him while the two other girls stayed with their mother for the entire week, rather than having all three children spend a few days together with each parent.

Given the family's terrible situation and the constant disjointed developments within our treatment framework, we decided that instead of going to the social service and the court, we would confront this pathological regression therapeutically. We therefore resummoned all three daughters with one parent to separate sessions, in which we brought up the most worrisome things about each girl. The eldest, Patrizia, seemed highly reactive, unmotivated about her schoolwork, and ready to hang out with the most disaffected adolescents. It was obvious that she was hurt by her father's indifference (he was totally preoccupied, first with his wife, then with Giada) and furious at receiving so little support from her mother. The second daughter, Simona, who was 13, had devised a strategy of withdrawal and silence, in which she went unnoticed; nevertheless, she suffered from constantly playing second fiddle to her sisters. Giada, in turn, acted closed and distant toward her mother and her sisters; she seemed incapable of finding her own self, an identity different from the ambiguous role of the Daddy's girl/Daddy's companion who was blatantly enamored of him. At a session involving the father and the three daughters, the therapist, after discussing Patrizia's and Simona's difficult situations, dwelled particularly on the risks to which Giada was exposed. With great frankness, she discussed the danger of incest developing in the little girl's relationship with her father. Among other things, the therapist emphasized that alcohol could weaken the inhibitions of the father, who already felt desperate because of his lonely existence.

Instead of changing his attitude, Mr. Laurieto became even more defiant: The following Saturday, he took Giada out of the institution and refused to bring her back—he was indifferent even to the fact that she was missing school. At the next session for the mother and the children, Giada was absent because her father would not bring her. The discussion zeroed in on the slavish conduct of the mother, who, to avoid making waves, had allowed her ex-husband to keep Giada for the whole of Easter week. She now apparently went along with the therapist's repeated comments about the little girl's dangerous situation. At this point, Patrizia reminded her of an episode that had occurred before the parents' separation: She had been sexually molested by her father. Then Simona backed up her sister by recalling a similar incident: She also had been molested a short time later. Faced with the therapist's serious and sympathetic bearing, the mother tried to justify the fact that she had never discussed this aspect of her husband's behavior. Still, she did accept the therapist's statements that it was necessary to report the matter to the police. After this clarification, Patrizia "recalled" two other instances of sexual advances from her father, which she had put out of her head.

During the next few days, the mother and the daughters did in fact go and bring charges against the father, while the therapist submitted a report to the judge. Finally, after several more days, the police removed Giada from her father's apartment, where she had spent over two weeks. She was placed in a center that was better equipped to deal with Mr. Laurieto's invasions.

At a session to which the father had been summoned individually, the therapist informed him with scrupulous precision about what had happened. Incredible as it may sound, this strengthened rather than weakened his intense dedication to therapy, which he pursued without its being mandated.

Meanwhile, Patrizia, during a visit to her mother's home, experimented with drugs together with a chronic drug addict; she was in a wretched state when she returned to her institution. After participating in a session with her mother and her sisters, she had several private meetings with the therapist. During these sessions, the exalted love that she declared for the drug addict was shown to be connected with the bitterness she felt toward her negligent mother. Mrs. Laurieto — after almost two years — stopped coming late to her sessions with her daughters, which alternated with individual sessions for Patrizia. The mother worked, with good results, growing closer to Giada and recognizing the emotional needs of both Patrizia and Simona.

We must also bear in mind that the girls felt guilty for reporting their father to the authorities; indeed, during her private sessions Patrizia talked about this at length. But now, the girls were able to cope with their guilt feelings more effectively and to work them out because of the therapist's good rapport with Mr. Laurieto, despite her role in denouncing him to the judiciary. This rapport presumably helped the girls to distance themselves temporarily from their father and to put off the necessary discussions with him to some future date when they would be less charged with tension.

The Sessions with the Couple

In line with what has been said so far, the reader must have grasped that when the therapist tries to eject an interfering third party—whether a child or a member of the extended family—from the conjugal relationship, the chief goal is, nevertheless, to help the couple's game unfold. The top priority of the entire therapeutic work is to aid the couple in achieving less pathological ways of functioning that do not lead to abuse or to the possible outbreak of a psychiatric symptom. Obviously, these more beneficial modalities can deepen the marital bond or else produce a separation that terminates the relationship, not only legally but also emotionally.

All other aspects of the game that are tackled in therapy are secondary to the couple's game, at which, in the final analysis, all the various therapeutic interventions are aimed. Granted, the sessions with members of the family of origin or with the nuclear family also deal with serious problems in the conjugal bond, and we do not necessarily have to isolate the two partners in sessions that are specifically reserved for them. But nevertheless, once the children have been dismissed, the subsequent therapy, as we have amply discussed, go to the very heart of the marital difficulties. In this phase of treatment, the most typical procedure in working with the couple—that is, the sessions with both partners—is used chiefly for cases in which the level of conflict is not excessively high. If too much hostility exists between the spouses, there is a risk that they may use the material of the session against one another. They may therefore remain extremely reticent during these meetings in order to avoid supplying weapons to the adversary. No sooner has one of them—perhaps at the therapist's urging—let slip any information than the other will seize on it to make accusations and blame the partner for ruining the family, abusing the children, causing the institutions to persecute the family, and so forth. The flames kindled at the meeting will continue to flare up, and the couple will rightfully maintain that the sessions only provoke them to fight even more.

In our caseload, we have seldom found spouses that fought so little as to make couple therapy superfluous. Yet not infrequently, after the larger sessions, the couple may find a point of cohesion, perhaps even form a coalition against a member of the extended family (as, say, in the case of Silvano and Giovanna, described in Chapter IV, p. 66). However, while playing upon this nascent togetherness, the therapist must exercise great caution in endorsing the "coalition against." The learning context of these families is so thoroughly permeated with violence that it can impel such a move toward extreme levels.

Even greater prudence must be shown in cases in which the parents ally themselves against one of their children. It can happen, when the spouses are playing a game in which one parent uses a child as an internal rival, that the child, from being the scapegoat for only the abusive parent, begins to arouse the hatred of the other parent, who has previously seduced her and instigated her against the spouse. In this connection, it is crucial that the therapist, while demonstrating the child's active moves in the game, prevent her changing from victim to persecutor. Instead, the therapist ought to show compassion and understanding for an eager child who is unwittingly drawn by adults into a game that is bigger than she.

The other target of a couple's coalition may be the therapist or the institutional system that he represents. However, this maneuver is seldom lasting; it functions purely as a lid forced upon a boiling pot and therefore it is certain to be blasted off very soon. If the therapist refuses to be discouraged by the wall that the two temporarily united spouses erect against him, he will find an aperture, no matter how small, into which he can squeeze and examine the game being played behind the wall.

We can cite an example of therapeutic work based on the couple's game by going back to the case of Laura and Igor and their very young parents, whom we talked about earlier in this chapter (pp. 154–157). The mutual aggression between the two young people, Ettore and Monica, diminished greatly when we laid bare the influence that Ettore's mother exerted on the couple. Her influence was all the sharper because Monica had lost her parents and she too, like Ettore, kept looking to her mother-in-law as an authority figure.

Once this obstacle was removed, the couple's game seemed to undergo a profound change on the surface. But the basic pattern remained unaltered. In fact, we noticed that Monica tended to lord it over Ettore, not only in front of his mother, but in front of all the important interlocutors: the social worker, our staff members, and even the therapist. It was also obvious that her attitude, rather than moving Ettore toward positive competition, inexorably pushed him toward the role of deviant that he had played for so many years.

Therefore, we looked for the roots of Monica's strategy within her learning contest. We had to understand why she refused to leave the husband who was causing her so much heartbreak, and why she kept showing him such inexhaustible patience with a slight tinge of superiority. We discovered that Monica's adolescence had been profoundly marred by her mother's alcoholism. The girl had greatly loved and admired her father; but, later on, she had accused him of causing his wife's depression and drinking problem with his extramarital affairs. Unlike her brothers and her older sisters, who very quickly lost interest in their mother's alcoholism, Monica, after her father's death, devoted herself body and soul to saving her mother. But she failed. "Now," the young woman confessed at an intensely emotional session, "I'm doing the same thing with Ettore. I want to change him, I want to redeem him. Every so often, I lose heart, but then I remember that he's younger than my mother was, which means I'll succeed. Sometimes, he raises my hopes. . . . He acts fine for a couple of months . . . but then he doesn't want to give me the satisfaction of having changed him!" Monica's penetrating observation signaled the start of her willingness to apply self-criticism. Pursuing this trail, the therapist worked on the collusive strategies employed by the two spouses—tactics that crystallized in their complementary roles with Monica as therapist and Ettore as patient. Within a short time, the two young people saw other possible modalities for a relationship.

Alternate Individual Sessions

For cases in which it strikes us as contraindicated to work with both spouses jointly, we resort to the format of two parallel individual treatments, usually conducted by the same therapist. Sometimes we have experimented with swapping the roles of direct therapist and supervisor for the two treatments.

As we saw in the Laurieto case, this is the choice to make for spouses who have separated but still maintain a high degree of emotional involvement. Often, the two treatments do not run for the same length of time; one of the two spouses may grow less and less committed to the therapy as the separation goes into effect. In such instances, the main work is pursued only with the other parent, who already has custody of the children or who stands a good chance of gaining it.

In these cases, the other spouse may decide both to drop out of therapy and to give up custody of the children. In that event, there is obviously a mutual influence between that decision and the team's decision to work more consistently and continually with the parent who seems more motivated to go through with treatment—and to get custody of the children.

We realize that in deciding to stop treatment, a parent cannot help being influenced by the therapist, even in a determining manner. However, in numerous cases, we felt we saw a powerful similarity between the parent's behavior in therapy and his or her behavior toward the child. There is the classical case of the father who lavishes gifts and attention on his child, hoping that this will help him get back his wife, who has left him. If his plan fails, then the father, in a subsequent phase, will pour out upon the child his anguish of abandonment and betrayal; he will even induce the child to exercise the close supervision over the mother that he, the ex-husband, cannot effectuate directly.

Such a father behaves quite analogously with the therapist. Although at first willing and helpful, he never enters into a real bond with the therapist to talk about himself and his own difficulties. On the contrary: he uses their meetings solely to glean information about his ex-wife or to recount, in his turn, episodes that may denigrate his wife in the therapist's eyes. Once he realizes that his strategy is not paying off, he tends to abandon both the therapist and the child.

At this point, the therapist must absolutely overcome the temptation to counteract with a hasty dismissal of the patient. Assisted by the team (which is less emotionally affected by the patient's refusal to go on with therapy), the therapist must at least try to motivate the father to accept his function as a parent, whom the child still vitally needs, even if he no longer lives with him. The therapist can be useful to the disappointed father, who is ready to drop his child once he loses all hope of getting his wife back. To help him, the therapist can offer to continue the relationship with him through dialogues for monitoring and for psychoeducational support. Their conversations may be less frequent and less profound than the therapist's conversations with the other spouse, but nevertheless they will be confidently proposed.

However, the therapist's relationship with the unwilling father remains precarious, and the latter's commitment usually fades, particularly when an eventual partner of the ex-wife joins her private sessions. In fact, should the wife involve a new companion in her relationship with her son, it may prove necessary to invite the companion to her sessions. This step normally functions as a signal that confirms the reconstitution of a new nuclear family and also induces the father to terminate therapy. If, however, the father does not simultaneously abandon his child, then the therapist's work, aimed at making the man's rapport with his child stronger and more authentic, will not have been in vain.

The formula of two alternating individual treatments is indicated not just for spouses who have separated. It functions remarkably well if the partners, in a couple session, are so afraid of exposing themselves to one another that they refuse to join with the therapist in confronting their interactive strategies. However, although these spouses may then come for individual sessions, they are nevertheless still undergoing a couple treatment and not true individual treatment. The latter is not feasible when the link with the therapist is still weak and the motivation for therapy quite instrumental. As we have repeatedly emphasized, although sessions involving several family members may be fruitful even when their participation is due chiefly to a court mandate, individual treatment requires personal motivation. We must remember that, if alternating individual sessions are called for, each partner is aware that the other is being treated in parallel appointments with the same therapist. This can induce the couple to develop a competitiveness that reinforces an uncertain motivation. Indeed, it is quite unlikely that either partner will feel like leaving a therapy aimed at resolving the crisis that led to the removal of their children. The therapist therefore has at his disposal several sessions to arouse a more genuine motivation. Nevertheless, the therapist may have to deal with resistance as expressed in the sentence, "He's the one who needs treatment, what am I doing here?" Or else a spouse may try to use the session purely to talk about his or her partner.

As for the question of what the therapist should tell each spouse about the material that has emerged in the other spouse's sessions, we have learned that this problem is less thorny than it might seem. Both partners are aware that the therapist possesses all the facts about the couple's game, that is, both versions, which are also enlightening about their various strategies. Usually, the therapist does not transfer the contents of a session to a partner's session, and she assures each patient that she will not do so. But sometimes, she asks one partner for permission to inform the other about an element that strikes her as particularly significant. In general, this occurs when there is little direct communication between the two spouses, who are extremely reluctant to expose themselves, dreading frustration and disappointment. As a result, the therapist must shed light on vast areas of their relationship that are crudely based on misunderstandings. In these cases, the therapist, seeking to overcome their reticence with one another, serves as a "telephone line" between the two frightened interlocutors.

We have often used this therapeutic format if one partner is alcoholic—which is often true of couples being treated at an abuse center. When the problem of alcoholism is the chief bone of contention in a marriage, it can scarcely be treated in joint sessions: The alcoholic stubbornly denies that he drinks too much, or else he minimizes the scope of his addiction, while his partner stubbornly tries to make him confess his vice. This situation greatly handicaps the therapy.

If the nonalcoholic partner is shown to have a behavioral element that may sustain the other partner's symptom, then the alcoholic may pounce on it as an excuse to continue drinking. On the other hand, the therapist may challenge the alcoholic's decision to drink, and she may suggest alternate strategies in his relationship with his partner. But then the latter can use the therapist's words against the alcoholic, throwing them up to him, telling him that his choice of drinking in order to make the partner suffer is a sign of his wickedness.

An example of these dynamics was offered by the Cividali family. This financially secure, middle-class family ran a family business. The parents, after years of marriage, had had only one child, Daniela, who was 11 at the time of the judicial intervention. The court had to step in because of family crises triggered by the mother's alcoholism. The yelling of the three members of the family had often induced neighbors to call the police; they, in turn, eventually notified Juvenile Court about the state of anguish in which they had found the girl—a spectator of family brawls that reduced the apartment to a battlefield. Daniela was now turned over to the child welfare office, which placed her in a semi-boarding school that allowed her to go home in the evenings. The tragedy had reached its peak several months earlier when the mother, trying to retrieve some household items that she had hurled from the balcony to an adjacent terrace, had plunged down to the courtyard, breaking both legs.

The initial sessions were limited to the nuclear family because Daniela's paternal grandmother, a key figure, was too sickly to attend. In the course of several months, these meetings, followed by those with the couple alone, brought to light two central issues.

The first issue was Mr. Cividali's intense bond with his mother, with whom he had lived for 30 years; she had been widowed at an early age when her husband had died of alcoholism. Mr. Cividali, a chronically depressed introvert, had found in his wife a woman who animated him with her exuberant character. However, he ran over to his mother every day, not only because she shared the management of the business, but also because he saw her as an oasis of calm and solace. He could thus escape the intrusions and impetuousness of his wife, who was profoundly jealous of his devotion to his mother.

The second issue was the position assumed by Daniela, who openly sided with her father. Her alliance might have been understandable had it begun with her mother's alcoholism. In fact, the girl depicted her father as the innocent victim of a drunkard who neglected the house and subjected him to endless unjustified scenes because he ate meals with his mother. However, the father-daughter alliance had long preceded Mrs. Cividali's alcoholism, adding more fuel to her acute jealousy. The mother, as is typical of alcoholics, denied having a drinking problem, though she owned up to drinking in the past—and she dramatically affirmed that she had decided to drink in order to kill herself, thereby punishing her husband and Daniela.

The exposure of the family game brought no significant change. The two spouses were totally preoccupied with scoring points against one another in front of the therapist, whom they used as an umpire: "You can see that she drinks." "You can see that it's his fault that I started drinking." After a few months of basically useless sessions, the bone of contention became Alcoholics Anonymous: The husband obstinately tried to drag his wife to their meetings, while she just as stubbornly dug in her heels and refused to go.

The turning point came when the therapist began seeing them separately. The husband's treatment focused on his depressions and the consequent necessity of seeking help by attending Al-Anon meetings.

This work produced rapid results. Mr. Cividali successfully participated in the group and made notable progress toward overcoming his depression. The therapist then immediately reduced the frequency of his sessions to keep from interfering with the exculpating message that Alcoholics Anonymous sends to relatives of alcoholics ("Alcoholism is a sickness"). At the same time, Mr. Cividali was asked by the group to take some responsibility: "If you want to help your wife, you have to change yourself."

Treatment for the wife had a very different thrust. It aimed at reconstructing her own family background, whose vicissitudes (which we will not go into here) predisposed her to getting herself adopted by her future mother-in-law. The wife tranquilly confirmed the therapist's supposition that she had married her husband in order to have his mother. She thus had two reasons for being jealous of Mr. Cividali's closeness to his mother, a relationship that survived despite everything. The wife suffered because her husband gave top priority to his mother and because she herself had failed to win first place in her mother-in-law's heart, even though she would lovingly tend her whenever she was bedridden. Still, she had ulterior motives for seeking the love of her mother-in-law: Her own mother had always been cold to her, and she wanted to make her jealous.

As the focus of treatment gradually shifted from the wife's relationship with her husband to her relationship with the important women in her life, the sessions became more fruitful. During the next few months, Mrs. Cividali resumed her interrupted relations with her maternal aunts and female cousins. However, it was harder mending her relationship with Daniela, who had meanwhile absorbed her father's pattern of instigation. The little girl was now a real provoker, filled as she was with resentment toward her mother for neglecting both her husband and her daughter and bringing shame on the family.

In the course of a final drunken and noisy scene, the wife herself called the social worker, who, with the court, saw to it that Daniela no longer came home at night. During a tempestuous therapy session, the father eventually managed to accept the judge's decision, thus breaking the chain of reprisals. With Daniela gone from home, Mr. Cividali succeeded in convincing his wife that his desire to see her cured of drinking was genuine and a sign of his real attachment to her. At the next session, his wife arrived in a state of poignant happiness after attending three Alcoholics Anonymous meetings.

The Rehabilitative Work

In the course of many months, our treatment program, which was integrated with and complemented by the intervention of Alcoholics Anonymous, led to a radical improvement of the situation of the Cividali family. This case allows us to introduce the theme of rehabilitative work, which has only recently become part of our team reflections.

For years—as we have already stated in this chapter—we ascribed too much power to the exposure of the game and to the other interventions characteristic of family therapy. Back then, we assumed that the break of a repetitive pathogenic game leads in and of itself to a new modality of functioning, which prevents the reappearance of both abuse and other signs of mental disturbance. Our ingenuously faithful opinion, among other things, contradicted previous experiences (Masson, 1981), which stressed the importance of a "reconstructive" phase for reorganizing the family in a new and "healthier" game that would be more satisfying for all the members.

Our eyes were opened by several dramatic relapses into abusive behavior, which we discovered when following up on families we had treated. These events, although not tragic, made us realize that our work was only half completed (Covini, 1985).

Undeniably, we had had several particularly fortunate cases of families, which, upon seeing each member's covert strategies, were able to discard their pathogenic conduct almost immediately. Sometimes this improvement took place through a (not merely legal) dissolution of the couple's bond, which was never assumed as a privileged relationship in regard to each partner's loyalty to his or her family of origin. In other instances, however, a marriage was given a radically new foundation, and the couple did not have to be subsequently accompanied when they renegotiated the rules of their marital and parental relationships.

The swift resolutions of such cases were probably aided by the judicial context (removal of children, penal sanction, etc.), which decisively drove these particular families to get out of their violent and abusive predicaments. In other instances, however, the various members of a family nucleus came up against tremendous obstacles as they struggled to find new ways of living together. There were many such hurdles: the inertia of rules that had consolidated over many years; the stranglehold of inadequately severed ties with persons outside the family; the social isolation caused by incurring the rigors of the law; the weakening of parental authority, which is inevitably harmed by sanctions; and the concomitant risk of the instigation of children against parents. All these factors can push a family back into preexisting organizational modalities.

Upon noting these processes, we refocused our attention on the phase of rehabilitative work, which begins after the phase of therapy per se is completed. We therefore maintain that for many cases, especially chronic cases and cases poor in resources—intellectual, cultural, economic, etc.—it is essential that the therapy phase be followed by reconstructive work. This process accompanies and continues the destructive effect that the disclosure of the game has exerted on any existing dysfunctional patterns. Interestingly enough, as we gradually realized that we had to keep up with a family long after the exposure of its game, our conviction was mirrored elsewhere. We are referring to the analogous revision of the goals and methods of family therapy in other contexts, for example that of the district psychiatrist (Selvini et al., 1987).

For each individual case, we have to pinpoint the persons or organizations that can supply this rehabilitative help. Alcoholics Anonymous does an excellent job in this connection: It offers an extremely tight and readily available network of relationships as well as a number of occasions—including social ones—that help the abusive family get out of its isolation. Furthermore, Alcoholics Anonymous encourages its members to recover or develop social abilities that our patients often utterly lack. For example, the capacity to make amends to people who have been mistreated or offended, to learn how to apologize, to learn how to ask forgiveness, etc.

In other instances, our Center, or a similar one, takes over the role of educating and rehabilitating parents, as in the previously illustrated case of Monica and Ettore. Both of them had grown up in seriously deprived families: She was the daughter of an alcoholic mother, and he, from earliest childhood, had been forced to steal by his greedy and despotic mother. For those reasons, both youngsters had no frames of reference in regard to proper upbringing. Although Monica, as we have said, tended to use our residential workers' suggestions to act superior to her husband, both spouses very quickly learned various kinds of educative behavior to implement with their children, all of which brought great satisfaction to Laura and Igor and to their parents.

In this regard, we ought to bear in mind that if children spend a long period at an attentive and caring center, they will then more easily detect parental conduct that strikes them as lack of interest and as neglect. These children will not infrequently say things like:

"Why don't you give me a good-night kiss? My residential worker always did!" Or "Why don't we all eat at the table? It was much nicer at the center!" In this way, a number of parents are surprised to discover behavioral standards of which they were completely unaware. This was true of a young father whose three children had been assigned by an institution to spend weekends with three separate families. Although offended by these measures—as the caseworkers expected—he exclaimed: "I wish I too had a family to go to."

In some instances, the reconstructive work can readily be done by the district social worker if she has maintained a consistent rapport with the family rather than simply monitored them. On the other hand, we have found that it is harder to refer patients to another therapist once we have concluded our treatment of the family games. Such a reassignment could pigeonhole the subsequent treatment as second-degree work, which, obviously, no one cares to go through with. Inevitably, when the therapist who is put in charge of rehabilitation faces such a predicament, he tends to discuss the work done in the preceding phase. He evaluates the inevitably partial results of the earlier treatment as unsatisfactory, thereby assuming an attitude of criticism and disapproval in regard to the client. As a result, the latter will soon stop coming to the agency and will risk a relapse into abusive behavior.

To forestall this danger, we decided that for lack of viable alternatives, we ourselves have to do the work of reeducating and rehabilitating parents after treating their family games. It therefore becomes our job to involve the clients in the process of acquiring new ways of relating and perhaps even help them to widen the range of behavior that they have taken on in the context of learning. This range is often tragically reduced in cases of individuals who themselves come from gravely pathological families.

No doubt, these initiatives, introduced by groups of abusive parents in other countries, following the model of Alcoholics Anonymous, would be extremely beneficial in this phase of treatment. For now, however, a well-thought-out organization of these types of intervention will have to wait for future programs.

REFERENCES

Allen, R., & Oliver, J. M. (1982). The effects of child maltreatment on language development. *Child Abuse and Neglect, 6,* 299–305.

Ammanniti, M., Matassi, R., Salomè, G., & Tolino, G. (1981). *Il bambino maltrattato.* Rome: Il Pensiero Scientifico.

Azzoni, M., Cirillo, S., Di Blasio, P., Frigerio, A., Gabbana, L., & Vassalli, A. (1985). La presa in carico coatta nei casi di maltrattamento dei bambini in famiglia. In S. Lupoi, A. De Francisci, & C. Angiolari, *Le prospettive relazionali nelle istituzioni e nei servizi territoriali.* Milan: Masson.

Bagley, C., & McDonald, M. (1984). Adult mental health sequelae of child sexual abuse, physical abuse and neglect in maternally separated children. *Canadian Journal of Community Mental Health, 3,* 15–26.

Bandini, T., & Gatti, U. (1987). *Delinquenza giovanile.* Milan: Giuffrè.

Barahal, R. M., Waterman, J., & Martin, H. P. (1981). The social cognitive development of abused children. *Journal of Consulting and Clinical Psychology, 49,* 508–516.

Bertalanffy, L. von. (1968). *General system theory* (rev. ed.). New York: George Braziller.

Bertotti, T., & Malacrea, M. (1987). Bambini maltrattati, piaga vergognosa della società moderna. *Vivereoggi, 4,* 25–40.

Bianchi, B., & Rangone, G. (1985). Maltrattamento infantile e intervento nei servizi pubblici. *Prospettive Sociali e Sanitarie, 14,* 8–10.

Bocchi, G., & Ceruti, M. (Eds.). (1985). *La sfida della complessità.* Milan: Feltrinelli.

Bolton, F. G., Reich, J. W., & Gutierres, S. E. (1977). Delinquency patterns in maltreated children and siblings. *Victimology, 2,* 349–357.

Boscolo, L., Cecchin, G., Hoffman, L., & Penn, P. (1987). *Milan systemic family therapy: Conversations in theory and practice.* New York: Basic Books.

179

Boszormenyi-Nagy, I., & Spark, G. (1973). *Invisible loyalties*. New York: Harper & Row.
Bowlby, J. (1984). Violence in the family as a disorder of the attachment and caregiving systems. *The American Journal of Psychoanalysis, 44*(1), 9–27.
Bowman, E. S., Blix, S., & Coons, P. M. (1985). Multiple personality in adolescence: Relationship to incestual experiences. *Journal of the American Academy of Child Psychiatry, 24*, 109–114.
Brassard, M. R., Germain, R., & Hart, S. N. (1987). *Psychological maltreatment of children and youth*. New York: Pergamon Press.
Brown, S. E. (1984). Social class, child maltreatment, and delinquent behavior. *Criminology: An Interdisciplinary Journal, 22*, 259–278.
Browne, D. H. (1988). High risk infants and child maltreatment: Conceptual and research model for determining factors predictive of child maltreatment. *Early Child Development and Care, 31*, 43–53.
Byrne, J. P., & Valdiserri, E. V. (1982). Victims of childhood sexual abuse: A follow-up study of a non-compliant population. *Hospital and Community Psychiatry, 33*, 938–940.
Camblin, L. D. (1982). A survey of state efforts in gathering information on child abuse and neglect in handicapped populations. *Child Abuse and Neglect, 6*, 465–472.
Canevaro, A. (1988). Crisi matrimoniale e contesto trigenerazionale. Un modello sistemico di terapia breve. In A. Andolfi, C. Angelo, & C. Saccu (Eds.), *La coppia in crisi*. Rome: I.T.F.
Child sexual abuse within the family. (1984). London: The Abe Foundation.
Cicchetti, G., & Rizley, R. (1981). Developmental perspective on the etiology, intergenerational transmission, and sequelae of child maltreatment. *New Direction for Child Development, 11*, 31–55.
Cigoli, V. (1983). Teorie e consuetudini come fonte di problemi: Verso una perizia sistemica. In V. Cigoli, G. Gulotta, & C. Santi, *Separazione, divorzio e affidamento dei figli*. Milan: Giuffrè.
Cirillo, S. (1986a). Dietro un bambino maltrattato c'è una famiglia in crisi. *Attraverso lo Specchio, Revista di Psicoterapia Relazionale, 14*, 18–22.
Cirillo, S. (1986b). *Famiglie in crisi e affido familiare: Guida per gli operatori*. Rome: La Nuova Italia Scientifica.
Cirillo, S. (1988). Affidamento familiare e presa in carico della famiglia: L'esperienza del CBM. In B. Barbero Avanzini & F. Ichino Pellizzi (Eds.), *Maltrattamento in famiglia e servizi sociali*. Milan: Unicopli.
Cirillo, S. (1990). *Il cambiamento nei contesti non terapeutici*. Milan: Rafaello Cortina Editore.
Cirillo, S., & Di Blasio, P. (1988). Revisione del concetto di ciclo ripetitivo della violenza. In V. Mayer & R. Maeran (Eds.), *Il laboratorio e la città* (Vol. 1). Milan: Guerini e Associati.
Cirillo, S., Di Blasio, P., Malacrea, M., & Vassalli, A. (1990). La vitimma come attore. In M. Malacrea & A. Vassalli (Eds.), *Segreti di famiglia*. Milan: Rafaello Cortina Editore.

Cirillo, S., & Sorrentino, A. M. (1986). Handicap and rehabilitation: Two types of information upsetting family organization. *Family Process, 25*, 283–292.

Council of Europe. (1981). *Criminological aspects of the ill-treatment of children in the family* (Vol. 18). Strasbourg: Council of Europe.

Covini, P. (1985). *La violenza in famiglia*. Unpublished thesis. Catholic University, Milan

Covini, A., Fiocchi, E., Pasquino, E., & Selvini, M. (1984). *Alla conquista del territorio*. Rome: La Nuova Italia Scientifica.

Crivillé, A. (1987). *Parents maltraitments, enfants meurtris*. Paris: Les E.S.F.

Crozier, M., & Friedberg, E. (1980). *Actors and systems* (A. Goldhammer, Trans.). Chicago, IL: University of Chicago Press.

De Lozier, P. P. (1982). Attachment theory and child abuse. In C. M. Parkes & J. Stevenson-Hinde (Eds.), *The place of attachment in human behavior*. New York: Basic Books.

Deschamps, G., Pavageau, M. T., Pierson, M., & Deschamps, J. P. (1982). Le devenir des enfants maltraités. Étude psychologique 7 ans après les services. *Neuropsychiatrie de l'Enfance et de l'Adolescence, 30*, 671–679.

Di Blasio, P. (1987). Denied coalitions. In M. Selvini Palazzoli, L. Anolli, P. Di Blasio, L. Giossi, I. Pisano, C. Ricci, M. Sacchi, & V. Ugazio, *The hidden games of organizations*. New York: Pantheon.

Di Blasio, P. (1988a). La promozione della salute nei casi di maltrattamento all'infanzia. In M. Bertini (Ed.), *Psicologia e salute*. Rome: La Nuova Italia Scientifica.

Di Blasio, P. (1988b). La diagnosi della famiglua maltrattante. In V. Mayer & R. Maeran (Eds.), *Il laboratorio e la città* (Vol. 2). Milan: Guerini e Associati.

Di Blasio, P., Fischer, J. M., & Prata, G. (1986). The telephone chart: A cornerstone of the first interview with the family. *Journal of Strategic and Systemic Therapies, 5*(1–2), 31–43.

DiNicola, V. F. (1990). Contrasting visions from Milan: Family typology vs. systemic epistemology. *Journal of Strategic and Systemic Therapies, 9*(2), 19–30.

Elmer, E. (1978). Effects of early neglect and abuse on latency age children. *Journal of Pediatric Psychology, 3*, 14–19.

Foerster, H. von (1982). *Observing systems*. Salinas, CA: Intersystems Publications.

Friedrich, W. N., Einbender, A. J., & Luecke, W. T. (1983). Cognitive and behavioral characteristics of physically abused children. *Journal of Consulting and Clinical Psychology, 51*, 313–314.

Furniss, T. (1983). Family process in the treatment of intrafamilial child sexual abuse. *Journal of Family Therapy, 5*, 263–278.

Furniss, T. (1984). Therapeutic approach to sexual abuse. *Archives of Disease in Childhood, 59*, 865–870.

Furniss, T. (1985). Conflict-avoiding and conflict-regulating patterns in incest and child sexual abuse. *Acta Paedopsychiatrica, 50*, 299–313.

Gaensbauer, T. J., & Sands, K. (1979). Distorted affective communication in abused neglected infants and their potential impact on caretakers. *Journal of the American Academy of Child Psychiatry, 18*, 236–250.

George, C., & Main, M. (1979). Social interactions of young abused children: Approach, avoidance, and aggression. *Child Development, 50*, 306–318.

Gulotta, G. (1983). Separazione, divorzio e affidamento dei figli: Presente e futuro. In V. Cigoli, G. Gulotta, & G. Santi (Eds.), *Separazione, divorzio e affidamento dei figli*. Milan: Giuffrè.

Haley, J. (1963). *Strategies of psychotherapy*. New York: Grune & Stratton.

Haley, J. (1971). Toward a theory of pathological systems. In G. H. Zuk & I. Boszormenyi-Nagy (Eds.), *Family therapy and disturbed families*. Palo Alto, CA: Science & Behavior Books.

Hinchey, F. S., & Gavelek, J. R. (1982). Empathic responding in children of battered mothers. *Child Abuse and Neglect, 6*, 395–401.

Hoffman, M. L. (1979). Is altruism part of human nature? *Journal of Personality and Social Psychology, 40*, 121–137.

Hoffman, M. L. (1982). The measurement of empathy. In C. E. Izard (Ed.), *Measuring emotions in infants and children*. Cambridge, MA: Harvard University Press.

Ichino Pellizzi, F. (1988). Il trattamento giuridico in Italia dell'abuso intrafamiliare secondo il codice vigente e secondo auspicabili linee di riforma. In B. Barbero Avanzini & I. Ichino Pellizzi (Eds.), *Maltrattamento in famiglia e servizi sociali*. Milan: Unicopli.

Kempe, R., & Kempe C. H. (1978). *Child abuse*. Cambridge, MA: Harvard University Press.

Kempe, C. H., Silverman, F. N., Steele, B. F., Droegmuller, W., & Silver, M. K. (1962). The battered child syndrome. *Journal of the American Medical Association, 181*, 17–24.

Kienbergen Jaudes, P., & Diamond, L. J. (1985). The handicapped child and child abuse. *Child Abuse and Neglect, 9*, 341–347.

Kohlberg, L. (1976). Moral stages and moralization: The cognitive-developmental approach. In T. Lickona (Ed.), *Moral development and behavior: Theory, research and social issues*. New York: Holt, Rinehart & Winston.

Lynch, M. A., & Roberts J. (1982). *Consequences of child abuse*. London: Academic Press.

Main, M., & Goldwyn, R. (1984). Predicting rejection of her infant from mother's representation of her own experience: Implications for the abused-abusing intergenerational cycle. *Child Abuse and Neglect, 8*, 203–217.

Malacrea, M., & Vassalli, A. (Eds.). (1990). *Segreti di famiglia*. Milan: Rafaello Cortina Editore.

Malagoli Togliatti, M., & Rocchetta Tofani, L. (1987). *Famiglie multiproblematiche*. Rome: La Nuova Italia Scientifica.

Martin, H. P., & Rodeheffer, M. A. (1980). The psychological impact of abuse on children. In G. Williams & J. Money (Eds.), *Traumatic abuse and neglect of children at home*. Baltimore, MD: Johns Hopkins University Press.

Masson, O. (1981). Mauvais traitements envers les enfants et thérapies familiales. *Thérapie Familiale, 2*, 269–286.

Masson, O. (1988). Mandats judiciares et thérapies en pédopsychiatrie. *Thérapie Familiale, 4*, 283–300.

Mastropaolo, L., Pesenti, E., Rizzo Pinna, E., & Daglio, R. A. (1985). L'interazione consultorio-tribunale. Strategie sistemiche operative. *Terapia Familiare, 17*, 29–37.

Minuchin, S. (1974). *Families and family therapy.* Cambridge, MA: Harvard University Press.

Minuchin, S., Montalvo, B., Guerney B., Rosman, B., & Schumer, F. (1967). *Families of the slums: An exploration of their structure and treatment.* New York: Basic Books.

Monane, M., Leichter, D., & Lewis, D. O. (1984). Physical abuse in psychiatrically hospitalized children and adolescents. *Journal of the American Academy of Child Psychiatry, 23*, 653–658.

Moro, C. A. (1988). Disturbo mentale del genitore e valutazione giuridica delle sue capacità educative. In M. Malagoli Togliatti (Ed.), *Disagio mentale e validità genitoriale.* Milan: Giuffrè.

Morris, M. G., & Gould, R. W. (1963). Role reversal: A necessary concept in dealing with the battered child syndrome. *American Journal of Orthopsychiatry, 32*, 298–299.

Oates, R. K., Forrest, D., & Peacock, A. (1985). Self-esteem of abused children. *Child Abuse and Neglect, 9*, 159–163.

Pardeck, J. T. (1988). An overview of child abuse and neglect. *Early Child Development and Care, 31*, 7–17.

Piaget, J. (1947/76). *Judgment and reasoning in the child.* Totowa, NJ: Littlefield, Adams.

Ponti, G. (1987). La perizia psichiatrica e psicologica nel quadro della legge penale. In G. Gulotta (Ed.), *Trattato di psicologia giudiziaria nel sistema penale.* Milan: Giuffrè.

Post, S. (1982). Adolescent parricide in abusive families. *Child Welfare, 61*, 445–455.

Prigogine, I., & Stengers, I. (1979). *La nouvelle alliance.* Paris: Gallimard.

Radke-Yarrow, M., & Zahn Waxler, C. (1976). Dimension and correlates of prosocial behavior in young children. *Child Development, 47*, 118–125.

Rheingold, H. L., Hay, D. F., & West, M. J. (1976). Sharing in the second year of life. *Child Development, 47*, 1148–1158.

Ricci, C. (1981). Interactional complexity and communication. In M. Selvini Palazzoli, L. Anolli, P. Di Blasio, L. Giossi, I. Pisano, C. Ricci, M. Sacchi, & V. Ugazio, *The hidden games of organizations.* New York: Pantheon.

Ricci, C., & Selvini Palazzoli, M. (1984). Interactional complexity and communication. *Family Process, 23*, 169–176.

Sack, W. H., & Dale, D. D. (1982). Abuse and deprivation in failing adoptions. *Child Abuse and Neglect, 6*, 443–451.

Sack, W. H, Mason, R., & Higgins, E. (1985). The single-parent family and abusive child punishment. *American Journal of Orthopsychiatry, 55*, 252–259.

Sagi, A., & Hoffman, M. L. (1976). Empathic distress in the newborn. *Developmental Psychology, 12*, 175–176.

Seel, B. F., & Pollock, C. B. (1968). A psychiatric study of parents who abuse infants and small children. In R. E. Helfer & C. H. Kempe (Eds.), *The battered child.* Chicago: University of Chicago Press.

Selvini, M. (Ed.). (1988). *The work of Mara Selvini Palazzoli*. New York: Jason Aronson.

Selvini, M., Covini, A., Fiocchi, E., & Pasquino, R. (1987). I veterani della psichiatria. *Ecologia della Mente, 4*, 60–76.

Selvini Palazzoli, M. (1970). Contesto e metacontesto nella psicoterapia della famiglia. *Archivio di Psicologia, Neurologia e Psichiatria, 3*, 203–211.

Selvini Palazzoli, M. (1974). *Self-starvation: From individual to family therapy in the treatment of anorexia nervosa* (Trans. A. Pomerans). New York: Jason Aronson. (Original work published in 1963)

Selvini Palazzoli, M. (1984). Review of B. Keeney, *Aesthetics of change*. *Family Process, 23*, 282–284.

Selvini Palazzoli, M., Boscolo, L., Cecchin, G., & Prata, G. (1984). *Paradox and counterparadox* (E. Burt, Trans.). New York: Jason Aronson.

Selvini Palazzoli, M., Boscolo, L., Cecchin, G., & Prata, G. (1980). Hypothesizing, circularity, neutrality: Three guidelines for the conductor of the session. *Family Process, 19*(1), 3–12.

Selvini Palazzoli, M., Cirillo, S., Selvini, M., & Sorrentino, A. M. (1985). L'individuo nel gioco. *Terapia Familiare, 19*, 65–73.

Selvini Palazzoli, M., Cirillo, S., Selvini, M., & Sorrentino, A. M. (1989). *Family games: General modes of psychotic processes in the family*. New York: W.W. Norton.

Selvini Palazzoli, M., & Prata, G. (1981). Le insidie della terapia familiare. *Terapia Familiare, 10*, 7–17.

Shengold, L. (1985). The effects of child abuse as seen in adults: George Orwell. *Psychoanalytic Quarterly, 54*, 20–45.

Soavi, O., & Vianello, O. (1990). Il contesto di controllo come possibilità di cambiare una famiglia in crisi. In S. Cirillo (Ed.), *Il cambiamento nei contesti non terapeutici*. Milan: Rafaello Cortina Editore.

Sorrentino, A. M. (1987). *L'informazione handicap*. Rome: La Nuova Italia Scientifica.

Speed, B. (1984). How really real is real? *Family Process, 23*, 511–517.

Toro, P. A. (1982). Developmental effects of child abuse: A review. *Child Abuse and Neglect, 6*, 423–431.

Vassalli, A. (1987). Bambini maltrattati e psicoterapia: Il trattamento coatto della famiglia. In W. Festini, C. Nosengo, & L. Saviane Kaneklin (Eds.), *Psiche e istituzione. Quali interventi clinci*. Milan: Angeli.

INDEX

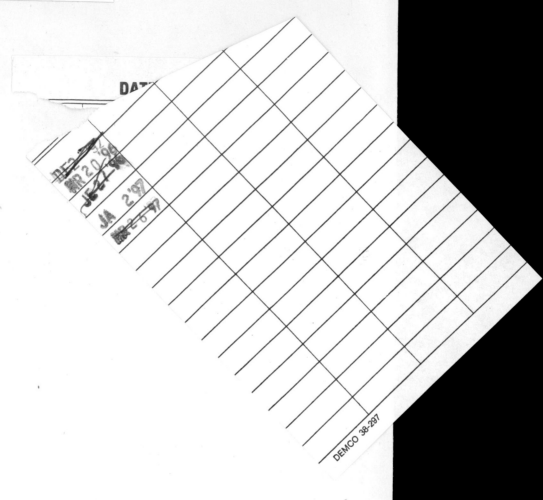

DEMCO 38-297